THOMAS HARDY
POET AND NOVELIST

Along the Froom

THOMAS HARDY
POET & NOVELIST

SAMUEL C. CHEW

878489

NEW YORK
RUSSELL & RUSSELL · INC
1964

To

L · E · C

In Memory of Our Visits

to Max Gate

OCTOBER, 1921

Preface

A few paragraphs in the following Study are reprinted from an article, "Homage to Thomas Hardy," published in The New Republic *of June 2, 1920, on the occasion of Mr. Hardy's eightieth birthday. For permission to include them here thanks are due to the editors of that journal.*

The writer desires to express his gratitude to Mr. Hardy for the permission, generously accorded, to quote such passages from his writings as were necessary to illustrate the points made in this book. These passages are taken from the definitive Wessex Edition of the Novels and Poems, published by Macmillan and Company.

S. C. C.

March, 1921

Note

The death of Mr. Hardy renders the present an appropriate time to re-issue, in revised and slightly enlarged form, this brief survey and estimate of his work. The original edition, now out of print, addressed to a smaller public than that which one now hopes to reach, appeared in the series of Bryn Mawr Notes and Monographs (*Longmans, Green and Co.,* 1921).

S. C. C.

January, 1928

Contents

THOMAS HARDY

I

Early Life

IN A SECLUDED Dorsetshire cottage, on the border of Bockhampton Heath about three miles from Dorchester, Thomas Hardy was born on the second of June, 1840. The house, a rambling seven-room structure, with gardens and with out-buildings now torn down, was built by his great-grandfather. Hardy's earliest extant poem, written about 1858, is a description of the home where he was then still living with his parents. In this piece, which with the title *Domicilium* was privately printed in 1918, there is evident feeling for the luxuriant loveliness of the surrounding beech-woods and for the desolate beauty of the nearby heath. His father was a master-builder or "contractor" (as we should say), employing about six workmen under him. The statement, still often met with, that Nelson's flag-captain was an ancestor of the novelist is incorrect; Captain Hardy belonged to another branch of the same stock. The Hardys are an old county family, formerly of importance but at the middle of the nineteenth century fallen in fortunes.

Thomas Hardy has mentioned them frankly as analogous to the D'Urbervilles in their decline from landed estate.

From his mother Hardy received his earliest education, supplemented presently by the instruction afforded by the Dorchester schools. The first impressions upon a mind unusually sensitive to surroundings were those of Nature and of the Past. Wandering over the heath behind the cottage, or through the woodland that partially enclosed it, beside the Froom and the Stour, within sound of the rushing weirs, among the apple-orchards and corn-fields, upon the lush, placid dairy-farms, in hamlets and larger villages, he observed not only the silence and the calm, but also the rivalry and the struggle of animal and vegetable life. The cruelty of Nature and her beauty impressed him deeply and the sense of this contradiction abides in his writings. All about him were memorials of the Past: Celtic, Roman, Saxon, Danish: venerable tracts of forest-land like the Chase in *Tess*, " where Druidical mistletoe was still found on aged oaks"; amphitheatre and round; earth-work, tumulus and fortress; Druid-stones and strange, rude monoliths whose origins were shrouded in mystery and festooned with folk-traditions. As a youth he must have often climbed about the gigantic, grass-grown slopes and entrenchments of Maiden Castle near Dorchester; and perhaps the very greatness of the impression produced upon his mind hindered him from turning this enormous relic of antiquity to imaginative account, for save in one brief sketch no scene of his stories is laid in the fortress. Like the older inhabitants of Casterbridge of whom he has written, he too may have seen within the Roman amphitheatre on the outskirts of the town " a gazing legion of Hadrian's soldiery as if watching the gladiatorial combat," a fleeting vision evoked by the intense imaginative appeal of the spot. And like his own Clym Yeobright, he must often have peopled the heaths with their ancient inhabitants. Like Clym, too, he picked up many a flint tool and arrow-head in the course of his wanderings. When, later in life, he built himself Max Gate, the house in which he lived for more than forty years, the excavation for the foundations laid bare pottery and jewelry of times long past, and in preparing a driveway workmen exhumed the skeletons of five Roman legionaries. In a tender little poem Hardy memorialized the maternal care that guided his stumbling childish feet along the Roman Road — the *Via* that is trodden by so many of the characters in the Wessex novels.

Thus life-long associations and age-long memorials bound Hardy's individual existence to the record of humanity. The very names of near-by places called up memories of " the long drip of human tears " and it was among such reminders of past civilizations that he spent his life. The peasantry of his youth-time had not yet learned to despise old ways and words. Then the molten image was still used to blast an enemy, and maidens still resorted to the woods of an Old

Midsummer-Eve in quest of a vision of their future partners for life. Fortunately for those who cherish such records and customs Hardy's young manhood came at a time when it was still possible to observe in abundance and to store away in memory for future chronicling many folk-survivals that were soon to begin to fade out before the sophisticating influences that have crept into the South of England. The repeal of the corn-laws, the introduction of railways, and later the enforcement of uniform education have brought changes into Dorsetshire and even before the Great War old customs and traditions and landmarks and types were fast disappearing. What " progress " had not entirely accomplished by 1914 the ruthlessness of military " necessity " then thoroughly performed, if we may judge by the fact that a recent pilgrim to Wessex found one of the heaths that served as a model for Egdon torn and scarred, the ancient ways defiled, the furze-bushes uprooted, and the barrows desecrated by multitudes of " tanks."

Around the young Hardy were reminders of a more recent Past. Then Waterloo veterans were still to be met with. There were vivid recollections of the stirring days when " there were two arch-enemies of mankind — Satan as usual, and Buonaparte, who had sprung up and eclipsed his elder rival altogether." The threat of Napoleon's invasion left an impression upon the Channel counties of a depth to which the Midlands and the North afford no parallel. Ruined huts on high points of land still marked the places where

dwelt the beacon-keepers who should signal the landing of the French. The seeds that half a century later
brought forth the magnificent literary fruitage of
The Dynasts were sown in Hardy's mind in his childhood. These early memories were reinforced some
years later when as a young man Hardy used to listen
to the yarns told by the Waterloo pensioners at
Chelsea.

Other vestiges of the comparatively recent Past
— Georgian residences, fragments of Elizabethan
manor-houses, old inns, barns that had once been
portions of old conventual groups, ruined abbeys, and
a multitude of churches that were soon to undergo
" the tremendous practical joke " of restoration —
must have helped to turn his mind towards the profession which at the age of sixteen he adopted and
which left so marked an imprint upon his books. In
1856 Hardy became a " premium pupil " of an architect named Hicks at Dorchester. It was the period
of the English Gothic Renaissance. As a secondary
result of the Tractarian Movement old churches,
crumbling and often crude enough, but interesting
memorials of local faith and local art, were being
" battered past recognition in the turmoil of the so-
called restoration." Like Ruskin, Hardy protests re-
peatedly in his books against this lack of reverence,
knowledge and good taste. The architect under whom
he studied was commissioned to superintend a good
deal of such reconstruction, and Hardy was sent to
sketch and measure many such edifices before their

old, familiar lines disappeared forever. The frequent journeys that these tasks necessitated helped to familiarize him with the country-side. The study and practice of architecture gave to the author of the Wessex novels, it is not fanciful to say, his evident grasp of the essentials of proportion, design, finish, selection, and exactitude. The structural excellence of the plays of Sir John Vanbrugh affords a like instance of the influence of strict training in design upon a literary artist. More obvious traces of Hardy's early profession are the detailed and at times too technical descriptions of the buildings in and around which his scenes are laid. Thence too comes, less happily, a crowd of similes and comparisons.

These were years of study far beyond the boundaries of his chosen calling. There is evident self-portraiture in some of the characteristics of Clym Yeobright and Angel Clare, young men upon whose brows thought has too early set furrows. There was no insuperable difficulty in the way of his going to one of the universities. The question was discussed in the family and particulars obtained from one of the Cambridge colleges. But in the end it was thought unnecessary for an architect. It is, therefore, incorrect to read any autobiographical hints into that yearning for academic distinction which is part of the tragedy of Jude Fawley. And, more fortunate than the obscure sojourner in Christminster, Hardy found in Dorchester a companion a little older than himself and, it is said, of more regular education, with whom he pursued studies in the classical and modern literatures and in theology.

It is impossible to determine the exact degree to which his studies of Greek literature influenced Hardy; but it is easy to see that from these studies come the Sophoclean tone of the greater novels, the power over Irony, the grasp of the principle of Total Effect, the ability to universalize the application of a contracted series of events. An intimate familiarity with the Bible, especially with the Old Testament, and, of the several books, especially with *Kings, Job,* and *Ecclesiastes,* turned now to serious, now to humorous purpose, pervades Hardy's writings. Knowledge of patristic literature and of modern theological disquisitions is evident in various places, especially in *Jude the Obscure* and in the extraordinary debate on baptism in *A Laodicean* (surely unique in romance among the methods whereby the hero comes to the aid of the damsel in distress). There is an oft-repeated anecdote of how Hardy about this time defended certain Anglican doctrines against strictures advanced by his unorthodox friends. Readings in English poetry stored his mind with the allusions, at times apt, at times rather forced, that recur constantly in the novels. With Wordsworth he had much in common and in Tennyson he must have found a sympathetic fellow-observer of the minutiae of the natural world; but the general trend of his thought led him far away from Browning, and the references to all three in the novels are uniformly disapproving

[9]

in tone. Allusions to Swinburne occur constantly and it is evident that *Poems and Ballads* and *Songs Before Sunrise* were influential in his intellectual growth. Hardy has himself admitted that the poetry of Crabbe helped suggest to him the choice of his subject-matter, but the outlook of the two men upon village and peasant life is in marked contrast. To Shelley go out Hardy's warmest tributes to an English poet; the Shelleyan conception of Love is found, as we shall see, in two of the novels. A minor poet who revealed to Hardy the almost untouched literary possibilities of Dorsetshire was his fellow-townsman William Barnes. After that poet's death Hardy published an obituary notice of him and many years later he edited a volume of selections from his verse, perhaps exaggerating the merits of his dialect poetry. Many other English poets are referred to from time to time: Shakespeare, Beaumont and Fletcher, Herbert, Milton, Congreve, James Thomson the First, Chatterton, Coleridge, Rossetti, Whitman — but without any particular significance attaching to the allusions. It is remarkable how free from literary traditions and schools Hardy's own verse is. The connection between his own early poetry and James Thomson's (" B.V.'s "), and Swinburne's is rather the result of independent minds being affected by the same tendencies in thought than of any closer bond of influence. There are, as has just been said, slight but definite connections with Crabbe and Barnes. But in so far as the literary ancestry of Hardy's poetry can be traced at all, the scant clues lead rather to the so-called metaphysical poets of the seventeenth century, especially John Donne, than to any writer of his own day. ⎍⎍⎍⎍⎍⎍⎍⎍⎍⎍

IN 1861 Hardy left Dorchester for the metropolis, there to study architecture under Sir Arthur Blomfield. While engaged in professional work he attended evening classes at King's College, thus rounding out his earlier, irregular education. In 1863 he won prizes for architectural theory and design from the Royal Institute of British Architects and from the Architectural Association. He widened his acquaintance with the other arts and in particular gained the familiarity with various schools of painting which he uses for purposes of comparison and description, now clumsily, now with exactitude and felicity, throughout his writings. In his first published novel, for example, may be found descriptions such as these: " A narrow, bony hand that would have been an unmitigated delight to the pencil of Carlo Crivelli "; and: " The reflection from the smooth, stagnant surface tinged his face with the greenish shades of Correggio's nudes." Mr. Penny, in *Under the Greenwood Tree,* is likened to " a framed portrait of a shoemaker by some modern Moroni." " The green lea," he writes in *Tess,* " was speckled as thickly with [cows] as a canvas by Van Alsloot or Sallaert with burghers." After his separation from Tess, Clare's attitude towards life is set before us thus:

[11]

Humanity stood before him no longer in the pensive sweetness of Italian art, but in the staring and ghastly attitudes of a Wiertz Museum, and with the leer of a study by Van Beers.

Among other artists whose works are alluded to here or there are: Raphael, Rubens, Greuze, Guido Reni, Turner, Terburg, Gerard Douw, Danby, Nicholas Poussin, Flaxman, Ruysdael, Rembrandt, Hobbema, Lely, Del Sarto, Spagnoletto, Sassoferrato, Reynolds, Carlo Dolci, and Sebastiano — the disregard of chronology and school in this list affording perhaps some indication of the range of Hardy's allusions. It is no mere parade of knowledge that Hardy offers, of course; rather it is an effort to present an exact pictorial description of persons and scenes; and as in the case of the crowd of similes drawn from architecture and from the world of nature, if he misses his mark, as occasionally he does, he falls into the awkward or the grotesque; but on the contrary, when successful, he brings home to the reader his scene or person with arresting vividness.

A promising career as an architect was opening before him. But already he was hesitating, uncertain as to the wisdom of his choice of a profession. Beyond doubt he puts his own experience into the mouth of Edward Springrove, one of the architects in *Desperate Remedies:*

Those who get rich [as architects] need have no skill at all as artists. — What need they have? — A certain kind of energy which men with any fondness for art possess very seldom indeed — an earnestness in making acquaintances, and a love for using them. They give their whole attention to the art of dining out, after mastering a few rudimentary facts to serve up in conversation.

Even before going up to London Hardy had begun to write verse and in London this occupation was continued. Again like Springrove, who was " a poet himself in a small way," he despised the " pap-and-daisy school of verse " — the allusion is obvious. " If anything on earth," Springrove remarks, " ruins a man for useful occupation, or for content with reasonable success in a profession or trade, it is the habit of writing verses." Fifty years later, in no such covert form, Hardy revealed the fact that he could find no publisher for the poems written during these years; and in *Who's Who* will be found the significant statement that he " had to drop verse for prose about 1868." It is said that many of these poems were afterwards destroyed. The themes of some, rewritten in prose, found their way into *Desperate Remedies*. But a large number of them, some in the form in which they originally stood, others revised, others built up from fragments and " old notes," have been given to the world during the last three decades. The quality of this work can be judged not only from the portion that remains, but from a description of the verses of Robert Trewe, the poet who figures in the short story of " An Imaginative Woman ":

He was a pessimist in so far as that character applies to a man who looks at the worst contingencies as well as the best in the human condition. Being little attracted by excellences of form and rhythm apart from content, he sometimes, when feeling outran his artistic speed, perpetrated sonnets in the loosely rhymed Elizabethan fashion, which every right-minded reviewer said he ought not to have done.

These sentences suggest, quaintly enough and with a characteristic tinge of irony, the characteristics of the writer's own early verse.

These thoughtful, sensitive and artistically immature poems exhibit the influence of the new forces which were changing the face of things in the sixties, destroying an old world while the new was powerless to be born, extending the life-history of mankind into " the dark backward and abysm of time," and peering out beyond what had once been the flaming ramparts of the world. The stronghold of orthodoxy was being assailed without and within. The Oxford meeting of the British Association and the publication of *Essays and Reviews* were events of the immediate past. The poetical atmosphere, among those who could not find refuge in a resurgent Cyrenaicism, became charged with pessimism, at times melancholy, at times in despairing revolt. Arnold voiced such feelings in "Dover Beach," and men found images of their own thoughts, cloaked in gorgeous Eastern drapery, in Fitzgerald's translation of Omar. In such a mood Swinburne inserted amid the earlier perfervid erotics of "Anactoria" the passage of flaming indignation against the gods that gives moral significance to the poem, and in the same mood wrote the middle choruses of *Atalanta in Calydon*. It was of such spiritual experiences that W. K. Clifford wrote a little later: " We have seen the spring sun shine out of an empty heaven, to light up a soulless earth; we have felt with utter loneliness that the Great Companion is dead." The despair of one such spirit is recorded in the majestic rhetoric of *The City of Dreadful Night*. Similar feelings lend a new depth to Ruskin's prose, in the preface to *The Crown of Wild Olive*. In this welter of conflicting purposes and ruined symbols some voices — Harriet Martineau's and George Eliot's, for example — were urging men to substitute, for duty to a dimly descried or altogether unknown God, the religion of humanity, the charity that " seeketh not her own." It was among these shaping influences that Hardy began to write.

Even in these early poems a preoccupation with the mystery of the world is seen shadowing Hardy's thought with what Meredith later called his " twilight view of life." This mystery is confronted from the point of view of one who is wont to analyze his own sensations and ideas. From the known microcosm of the poet's individuality he looks out upon the macrocosm, the Great Unknown. He finds no hint of orderliness in the universe; no sign of direction is apparent, no evidence of plan. Thus there begins the contrast, expressed so often in his writings, between the unweening Cause and the individual human consciousness that has somehow been evolved in certain of the creatures of that Cause. Very impressive is his cry for a First Cause, even malign, in place of the purposelessness of " crass Casualty." His is not the poetry of intellectual revolt like that of Swinburne; nor is his the merely puzzled and wandering mentality of such men as Clough. Hardy has already reached a negative position, like that of James Thomson, though in the occasional introduction of what looks like a malign fatalism there is evidence of repugnance to accept the evidence for mere determinism, a repugnance the more natural in a mind trained in such traditions of direction and plan as are given by architecture. One must note also that though the point of view is almost always that of Leopardi and of " B.V.," sheer personal ill luck has no part in framing Hardy's more generalized indictment of the world. And in this connection it may be said, once for all, that mere physical suffering plays a small part in his novels and poetry. Moreover, in contrast to such men as Beddoes, who revel in what may be called literary pessimism, there are already meditations upon the pathos of unbelief. The gayer and more humorous poems of Hardy belong for the most part to a later period of his life. Here broodings upon death are constant. In 1867 the grimly grotesque piece " Heiress and Architect " was written. The dedicatory initials that follow the title of this poem suggest a personal application, but beneath the individual experience there is certainly allegory; the heiress being a representative of humanity, full of hopes and ideals, and confronted

by the architect, " an arch-designer," who typifies the
rigor and indifference of the universe. One by one, as
she indicates now one plan and now another, he shat-
ters her illusions, until she pleads at last for a "narrow, winding turret," reaching to a loft where she
may sit alone and grieve:

> " Such winding ways
>   Fit not your days,"
> Said he, the man of measuring eye;
> " I must even fashion as my rule declares,
>   To wit: Give space (since life ends unawares)
>   To hale a coffined corpse adown the stairs;
>   For you will die."

The man who at the age of twenty-seven could write
this strange meditation upon the *Trionfo della Morte*
must have cast off many illusions. In this and in many
other poems there is a sense of *le grand sommeil noir*
that enfolds the little waking moment called life.
One feels in them a desolating consciousness of isolation — "Yes! in the sea of life enisled" — a consciousness of the impenetrable wall that shuts off
individual from individual. The island of life is com-
passed about by the sea of oblivion, and in certain
poems Hardy seems to cry with Leopardi: *E il nau-
fragar m'è dolce in questo mare!* In other poems
temporary joy is found in love and friendship. But
everywhere there is a complete repudiation of the
Carlylean remedy of action for despondency. Other

poems still, for despair is wont to veil itself in cynicism, are harsh in tone, distrustful of humanity, questioning its efforts and ideals in a manner out of accord with the essential sympathy and tenderness that, certain passages in the novels notwithstanding, are at the base of Hardy's view of life. Many poems are studies in the freaks and pranks of the " purblind Doomsters " who mismanage human fate. In all one finds already a refusal, characteristic of all his writings, of false consolation and empty hope; a determination to look at " the worst contingencies as well as the best in the human condition "; a deliberate and courageous posing of difficult questions. Here he differs from Clough and from the Arnold of the earlier years, who are groping and perplexed, anxious to retain emotionally the ideas and hopes that they repudiate intellectually. And Hardy's limitations are already as apparent as are his excellences. His steady view of life does not embrace the whole of life. It was not till towards the close of his career that he admitted (in the General Preface to the Wessex Edition of his works) that his was a nature becoming vocal at tragedy rather than at comedy. " The truths of midnight," as James Thomson admitted to George Eliot, " do not necessarily exclude the truths of noon-day." But from these early poems there is no evidence to be drawn that, though undemonstrative before a contrasting side of things, Hardy was not unperceiving.

2
A Survey of the Novels

In 1865 Hardy published in *Chambers' Journal* his first short story: "How I Built Myself a House." Here he employs in fiction for the first of many times his knowledge of architecture. He tells in humorous vein (suggesting the influence of Dickens) of the experience of a young couple who, dissatisfied with the villa in which they live, build a dwelling according to their own plans and specifications. In the course of its construction various improvements are worked into the original plans, and when at last it is finished they are by no means satisfied with it. The passage in which the supposed narrator describes his dizziness as he stands on the high scaffolding of the half-built dwelling and the warnings of the carpenter lest he fall, anticipates the use made of the same situation in the sensational accident at the beginning of *Desperate Remedies*. Notwithstanding the trivial humour of the story there is a duly subordinated suggestion of the futility of human efforts; the outcome of our plans rarely measures up to our expectations. Very seldom in later stories and never in the novels does Hardy employ the first-person form of narrative here used.

The distractions of literary pursuits and an inability to stoop to meretricious means of gaining patrons must have strongly affected Hardy's attitude towards architecture during his last years in London. He came to despise " society " (in the narrow sense of the term). A misunderstanding that is out of accord with his usual tolerance and sympathy towards humanity in general plays a part in this contempt. From his experiences in the social world are derived the feeble satiric sketches in the London portions of *A Pair of Blue Eyes* and the attempts, extraordinary only in their weakness, to portray that world in *The Hand of Ethelberta, A Laodicean, Two on a Tower*, and elsewhere. In 1867 he left London, settled at Weymouth, and began his first novel, while still practising his profession.

The Poor Man and the Lady was submitted to the publishing house of Chapman and Hall in the latter part of 1868. Many years later Hardy himself described this story as an incoherent production full of revolutionary and anti-social theories. According to the well-known anecdote, George Meredith, the publishers' reader, granted Hardy a personal interview and advised him to withdraw the manuscript; but there is some reason to believe that it was rejected outright. S. M. Ellis tells that at a meeting of a literary society in 1895 Meredith and Hardy both referred to this early association, Hardy describing his rejected first story as " very wild," whereupon Meredith called out: " Promising! " Forty years afterwards, when Meredith died, Hardy recalled the trenchant words, turning to kindness, of this interview. It is said that Meredith urged him to quit introspection and philosophizing in fiction and to try his hand at a novel of complicated intrigue. Hardy made no further effort to get *The Poor Man and the Lady* published. Till lately it survived in manuscript but is now destroyed.

ᴜᴜᴜᴜᴜᴜᴜᴜᴜ

HARDY followed Meredith's advice and, accepting frankly the code of the popular " sensation novelists " of the day, composed *Desperate Remedies*. There is no truth whatever in the statement occasionally met with that this book is a mere revision of his first rejected story. It is an entirely independent work of a quite different order. A companion error to the effect that this second novel was accepted on Meredith's recommendation is refutable by reference to any bibliography of Hardy. *Desperate Remedies* was published anonymously in 1871 by the firm of Tinsley Brothers. Hardy himself had to finance the undertaking and advanced seventy-five pounds for that purpose.

The writer of one monograph upon Hardy puts *Desperate Remedies* aside as a sort of *Titus Andronicus* among the Wessex novels, unworthy of any consideration. This is quite uncritical. It is an immature and in some respects disagreeable book, a tale of mystery, crime, startling coincidence, and melodramatic incident, which in its use of entanglement, suspense and moral obliquity reveals the strong influence of Wilkie Collins. Its opening words describe it as " a long and intricately inwrought chain of circumstance." Sensational incidents like the burning of the inn and the midnight burial indicate very definitely the indebtedness to Charles Reade and Collins. This is seen also in the ever-present intention to " keep the reader guessing," in the division of the events of the story according to periods of time, and in the written confession left by the villain of the piece, which turns up after his death. The portrayal of the brutal animalism of Manston's love for Cytherea is remarkably frank considering the date, as is the curiously morbid episode of Miss Aldclyffe's visit to Cytherea's room at night. These episodes seem to follow the lead of Reade's *Griffith Gaunt* (1866) in the effort to break through the conventions of Victorian prudery.

But though obviously the work of an imitator, the book offers, both in structure and in character-drawing, certain adumbrations of some of the most typical traits of the later novels. Hardy gradually abandoned the employment of mystery and suspense in favor of the equally effective and perhaps more philosophical method of tragic anticipation; but these cruder means of sustaining interest did not disappear immediately after *Desperate Remedies*. Already he exhibits his ability to weave a highly complicated plot while keeping a sure grasp upon every strand of the tangle of purposes and interests. There is little in the character of the heroine, except her inability to stand firm against external influences, to suggest the type of woman later peculiarly associated with Hardy; she is franker, less indirect, less subtle, and on the whole more stable. She and Miss Aldclyffe are immature studies in contrasting types of forcefulness and delicacy. The illicit love-affair of Miss Aldclyffe's youth is the first of many such incidents in the novels. Manston, her natural son, faintly suggests Hardy's most powerful study of a man in the grip of an overmastering passion — Boldwood. It is noteworthy that his temperament is in part accounted for by the circumstances of his birth. Contrasted with him is the less egoistical, more self-controlled Springrove. We have thus the beginnings of a theme to which Hardy often recurs: sensual selfishness against self-sacrificing devotion matched in a struggle for the possession of a loved woman. The two scenes mentioned above indicate the promise of great strength in depicting startling incident. But there is no sweetness in the book, and subtlety only in those passages which are obviously mere transcriptions of early poems. Such paraphrases often take the form of disconnected aphorisms of a philosophic sort and in sombre vein, generally stiffly and awkwardly expressed. But there is no large philosophic implication that raises the interest above the level attained by a merely ingenious plot. Beneath the conscientiously documented external "realism" of Budmouth and

Knapwater House there is a thoroughgoing romanticism of treatment; and even the realism of setting is of a sort that Reade could produce any day from his scrap-books and pigeon-holes. In this respect Hardy had a long way to go before he became master of the art that is visible in the living presentation of Dorchester in *The Mayor of Casterbridge*. An exception must be made, however, of the modest but convincing beginning of his transcripts of country life, in his reproduction of the dialogue and characteristics of the peasantry. The occasional rustic scenes — the inn-keeper and his friends, the postman, and the bell-ringers — are not only promising but excellent in themselves.

Though almost ignored by the public (a second edition was not called for until 1889), *Desperate Remedies* obtained some qualified praise from the critics. Indecision was expressed with regard to the author's sex, the knowledge of female character seeming to denote a woman, " the occasional coarseness of expression " a man. The West Country characters were singled out as the best part of the book by judicious reviewers, one of whom declared them to be " almost worthy of George Eliot."

This remark is the first appearance in print of an idea that has haunted critics of Thomas Hardy. Lately an entire book has been devoted to a comparison of him with George Eliot, the contrast there drawn being entirely in favor of the woman. But as a matter of fact the dissimilarities are far more marked than the resemblances. Each writer uses the novel as a medium for the communication of ideas, and in each the tendency to philosophize becomes more outspoken in later books. But the views of life that they set forth are poles asunder. The tragic conflict in George Eliot's conception is between desire and conscience; it is an internal war. Conscience plays a small part in Hardy's books. He envisages life as a struggle between will and destiny. Man is master of his fate in George Eliot; the problem is a moral one. Fate, according to Hardy, is beyond human control. The one preaches action and resistance; the other submission, quietism. In both writers hereditary taints and the contaminations of environment play a part; but in George Eliot their influence is preponderating, in Hardy they do not determine the outcome. Both introduce the rustics of their native counties into some of their novels, the yokels disappearing from George Eliot's later fiction as they do from *Jude the Obscure*. These peasant characters of equally remote districts naturally possess in common many traits of manners and beliefs. But the older novelist's carefully realistic studies of country life lack the lightness, relief, and flavour afforded by the undertone of quiet amusement which while it lessens the realism enhances the charm of Hardy's country scenes. There is little in common between Hardy's peasantry and George Eliot's small townspeople, though her success in delineating provincial types may have suggested to Hardy to turn to artistic account the customs and traditions of the Southron folk among whom he had grown up and whom he best knew. It has been suggested that Blackmore, too, whose *Lorna Doone* had appeared in 1869, may have helped to guide Hardy into Wessex; but this is unfounded, for at that time Hardy did not know Blackmore's tale.

At all events it was this vein of his genius, and quite evidently following the lead of George Eliot, that he worked exclusively in his next story, *Under the Greenwood Tree*, which was published anonymously in 1872. This is unpretentious in scale and theme and far removed from the complexities of *Desperate Remedies*. It is an intimate, detailed, humorous and delicately ironical story of a rural courtship. Then and until long afterwards it required, as one of Hardy's characters remarks elsewhere, " a judicious omission of your real thoughts to make a novel popular "; and it would have been a shrewd critic who could have detected at the time the undertone of bitterness in the portrayal of the indecision and deceptiveness of the winsome heroine, Fancy Day. It is, indeed, possible to exaggerate the significance of this undertone, for as a whole the tale is blithe enough. The simple love-story is set against a background of village life. It is, as the subtitle has it, " a rural picture in the Dutch School " and suggests some sweet orderly interior by Vermeer or De Hooch. The gloom of the early poems is put aside in the contemplation of these lives that accept with serenity the countless links that bind them close to Nature. Never, save in *Far from the Madding Crowd* and in some of the Wessex scenes of *The Dynasts,* has Hardy surpassed the quaint humour of the rustic talk. The original title of the book (preserved as a subtitle in recent editions) was " The Mellstock Choir." This is appropriate, for the comedy of Fancy Day's love-affairs is interwoven with the problem confronting the rustics of how to forestall or at least postpone the introduction of an organ-player in the village church in place of the time-hallowed west-gallery choir and band. This innovation, seemingly so unimportant, is typical of the revolutionary influences that were creeping into Wessex from the outside world. The choir's visit of protest to the vicar is unforgettable in its sweet good-humour, verging upon, but never quite degenerating into, farce. No less excellent are such scenes as that of the Christmas " wake " and the dance (the first of many dances in the Wessex novels) at William Dewy's. The tale is not, and does not pretend to be, a profound work of art. But the art, unpretentious as it is, is masterly; the charm, however homely, is inimitable; and there are more serious implications, perhaps, than appear on the surface.

The first book to bear Hardy's name upon its title-page was *A Pair of Blue Eyes* (1873). The obvious immaturity of this story has been admitted by its author. In the contrasting scenes of comedy and pathos there is evidence of the influence of Dickens, though the alternations are accomplished with more dexterity and refinement than the master was generally capable of. And too much of the influence of Wilkie Collins still remains. Sensational events and coincidences are too frequently resorted to in order to sustain the interest. It is unnecessary to set down here a full list of these devices, but the use of coincidences which in their number stretch to the limit the reader's willing suspension of disbelief is so significant for Hardy's development and philosophy that some notable examples must be given. Mr. Swancourt chose the same day for his secret marriage that his daughter selected for hers. The one person whom Elfrida and Smith met on their return from London was the old woman whose hatred of Elfrida made that meeting doubly unfortunate. Knight, the person who befriended Smith, was the reviewer of Elfrida's romance and was also the second Mrs. Swancourt's cousin. Elfrida found her missing ear-ring, looked for previously in vain, at precisely the most awkward moment possible. The church tower fell just after Elfrida had indicated it as the very symbol of steadfastness. Mrs. Jethway, Elfrida's enemy, was buried beneath its ruins. Knight and Smith, acting independently, returned to Devonshire by the same train that carried the body of their loved one. Chance is certainly overworked, and the artist, several times barely escaping the farcical, has not sufficient mastery to render acceptable so formidable a conglomeration of its freaks. But one must bear in mind the part that " Hap " plays in Hardy's scheme of things and perhaps regard these strangely juxtaposed events as extreme illustrations of the whimsicality of chance in disposing of human affairs. "Hap" does not change character; it alters the course of events. Moreover, the long chain of disastrous circumstances begins, not in chance, but in Elfrida's moral cowardice, her inability to clear up and make straight at once a disagreeable situation. In this moral cowardice Smith has his share. And we shall see later that it is in part responsible for the ruined lives of Tess and Jude. But in *A Pair of Blue Eyes* these shortcomings of character account only in part for the resulting tragedy. There are whims and aberrations of chance that are external to human character and irrespective of human effort. It is not merely in themselves that the personages of the story " are thus and thus "; the outcome is in part controlled by external circumstances, the meeting with Mrs. Jethway and the loss of the ear-ring for example. And, finally, it is not fantastic to suppose that Hardy's insistence upon the marvellous in coincidence is intended to take the place to some degree of the supernatural element of earlier fiction, Hardy's evident feeling for the supernatural being held in check by the rationalistic tendencies of his time. What he could do in the way of suggesting the supernatural, without yielding himself wholly to its fascination, may be seen in various later stories: in the short tale of " The Withered Arm " and in certain episodes of *The Return of the Native* and *The Mayor of Casterbridge*.

A Pair of Blue Eyes* marks a distinct advance

upon the two former novels. There was no telling that the author of *Desperate Remedies* would ever accomplish anything of genuine worth; and *Under the Greenwood Tree,* for all its charm, promises only such things as *The Trumpet-Major,* some of the short stories, and the rustic scenes in other books. The philosophic implications of the present story, on the other hand, are harbingers of many of Hardy's most mature ideas. Human action is seen to be fettered by Cause on the one side and by Effect on the other. The human will, thinking itself free, is nevertheless bound fast by the " purblind Doomsters " that unthinkingly ordain what is to be. The line of thought is similar to that of many of the early poems. The famous episode on the cliff when Elfrida saves Knight from a terrible death is the first full indication of Hardy's powers in swift, tense narrative. These powers of concentration upon essentials, of proper grouping of details, of imparting to the reader that same dread of immense height which one finds in the familiar lines in *King Lear,* need only to be expended upon less melodramatic themes to be first-rate. Several of the characters are noteworthy. Elfrida Swancourt is a clearly defined study of the type of woman faintly outlined in the sketch of Fancy Day: perilously attractive (irony lurks beneath the apparently trivial title of the book), indecisive, intellectually quick but shallow, not heartless but frail, impatient of opposition yet quite unable to face a situation determinedly. The creature of impulse, quick to respond to every wind of persuasion, she yet possesses a certain definiteness of character that anticipates with variations Bathsheba Everdene, the heroine of Hardy's next book. Smith, the young architect, is a slightly-drawn boyish figure. But Knight, the journalist, is the first of several thoughtful men in the novels who imagine themselves to be emancipated and liberal-minded but who are more enmeshed by tradition and convention than they are aware. The footsteps of such men are dogged by tragedy. Clym Yeobright belongs with this group; Angel Clare is the capital example of the type. Knight demands unsullied maidenliness in his bride; and when the indiscretions of Elfrida are revealed to him, his cloudy ideal, veiling the light of her essential purity, obscures the circumstances in which she had been entrapped. He leaves her. The story thus presents what Hardy later called " the romantic stage of an idea " used again in *Tess of the D'Urbervilles*.

A Pair of Blue Eyes takes the reader, in its setting, farther westward than do the other novels, to the wild country around "lone Camelford and Boscastle divine " which Swinburne has described in one of the most beautiful of his elegies. The carefully subordinated picture of the rustics gives a realism that the book might have lacked had it dealt only with the personages of a higher social stratum. One rustic scene, that in the church vault where the yokels are preparing for the burial of Lady Luxellian, is hardly to be matched in Hardy's writings for rich humour mingled with grimness. This episode, though touched with Shakespearean reminiscence, is drawn from memories of a scene actually witnessed by Hardy when a boy of fifteen. William Worm, Mr. Swancourt's man-of-all-work, is the first (except poor Thomas Leaf) of the thin-witted, slack-limbed, wambling fellows that are pitied and patronized by their sturdier associates.

The heroine is fashioned in part, as we know on good authority, from Hardy's future wife, Miss Emma Lavinia Gifford; the hero, though like Hardy an architect, is not "a portrait of the artist as a young man " but is drawn closely after a fellow-pupil in Hicks' office in Dorchester. A comparison of the descriptions of the country in which the comedy and tragedy of Elfrida's life and fate are played out and the reminiscences of the same landscape in the touching and curious poems written after the death of Hardy's first wife ("Poems of 1912-1913 ") will reveal some of the autobiographical touches in the tale.

What the novel lacks is just that quality that Hardy was later to possess to a degree equalled by no other English novelist: the ability to read into a series of happenings to a group of unimportant people in a remote district a universal application, a suggestion of the inescapable one-ness that enfolds all human affairs. The style, when it seeks to be urbane, is still often awkward and ungracious; sentiments intended to be of tragic import are generally merely harsh and bitter; the "strong" scenes sometimes overreach themselves and verge upon the ludicrous. But there is a sure command of his medium in the landscape drawing and in the dealings with the peasantry. On the whole there is a relapse from the flexible and confident grasp of *Under the Greenwood Tree;* but it is a relapse that comes from essaying a more difficult feat of the novelist's art.

A Pair of Blue Eyes was the first of Hardy's novels to appear in serial form before publication as a book. It appeared in *Tinsley's Magazine* between September, 1872, and July, 1873. Thereafter each of the novels, though often not in final form, was published first in one magazine or another. The success of this story was sufficiently marked to warrant Hardy's abandonment of architecture, and thenceforth he committed himself wholly to imaginative literature.

ᴗᴖᴗᴖᴗᴖᴗᴖᴗᴖ

AN invitation from Frederick Greenwood now resulted in the great popular success of *Far from the Madding Crowd,* which was published anonymously in the *Cornhill* during the whole of 1874. At the conclusion of its serial run it was issued in book-form with Hardy's name on the title-page. In the same year Hardy married Miss Gifford. He moved from Weymouth to Sturminster-Newton, thence to London for several years; later he removed to Wimborne, and finally in 1885 to the outskirts of Dorchester. For many years thereafter, however, it was his wont to take annually a house or flat in London for several

months. His active life was not spent so uninterruptedly in rural isolation as it was popularly supposed
to be.

In *Far from the Madding Crowd* many sides of
Hardy's genius are shown fully developed. There are
still the flashily sensational incidents of which he
never wholly rid himself, such as Troy's exhibition to
Bathsheba of his skill at the sword-exercise (a scene
much in the manner of Charles Reade) and the same
soldier's snatching of the note from his wife's hand
at the fair. The structural mastery is by no means
flawless. Nor is it typical of Hardy's art to leave a
loose end ungathered up as he does in the inconclu-
sive confinement of Boldwood in an insane asylum
" during her Majesty's pleasure." But the many excellences of the novel ensured not only its immediate success (which carried with it the inconvenience
of attaching to its author's name the reputation of
being a first-rate story-teller, thereby obscuring for a
generation his significance as a thinker) but its permanent place among the classics of the English novel.
These merits were especially the variety and vivacity
of the moods and interests; the power of devising a
series of convincingly connected yet surprising situations; the insight into character, especially the character of a certain type — for Hardy always the pre-
eminent type — of woman; the minutely detailed
and sympathetic nature-description in which the
interrelationship of man and the natural world is
brought out with a forcefulness that revealed to some

contemporary readers the significance of this connection in the author's view of life; and the passages of intensely vivid narrative such as the burning of the rick, the bringing home of Fanny's body, and the doings of the gargoyle during the rain-storm. In the picture of the shearing-supper — Oak piping on his flute while the shearers recline at their ease in the gathering twilight — a scene redolent of the bucolic tradition of all ages, Hardy almost transcends his medium and approximates to those effects of light and colour and composition that have been accomplished in the sister-art by such painters as Troyon and Rousseau. It must be admitted, however, that in Hardy's more highly finished landscapes there is a tendency to exaggerate their romantic qualities. In no other book are his peasants more delightful or their humour more fragrant; he has in great measure shaken off the too literary flavour, the suggestion of Shakespearean imitation, that to a certain degree harms the effectiveness of, say, the remarkable scene in the church-vault in *A Pair of Blue Eyes*.

The pervading theme of *Far from the Madding Crowd* is one that is to reappear with slight variations and subtle shiftings of emphasis in two later books and of which reminiscences are found in others still. The motive is that of the contrast between self-seeking unbridled passion and faithful, unselfish devotion, controlling not only judgment but emotion (which is a harder matter). The latter type of love is embodied in the shepherd Gabriel Oak. Some readers may observe a certain hesitation in the initial conception of his character; the picture of Oak with which the book opens presents a peasant who is rather more of a hind, rather more of an uncouth yokel, than Oak turns out to be. But probably, though this is not made very clear, it was intended that the maturing influence of misprized love and of financial ruin should be accepted as effecting the contrast between the shepherd of the first chapters and the shepherd of Bathsheba's farm. Those critics are in error who declare that Oak's character is undifferentiated from that of Venn in *The Return of the Native* and that of Winterborne in *The Woodlanders*. There are points of difference. Oak is more masterful, more confident than Giles; from the very beginning of the tale the reader experiences an undefined feeling that he will be able to work through his difficulties and disappointments to contentment. And he is a less mysterious figure than Venn, without the almost mystic temperament that leads Venn to adopt his queer calling after disappointment in love and that makes him, as it were, an incarnation of the spirit of Egdon Heath. But all three men, as well as John Loveday in *The Trumpet-Major*, are cast from the same mould. In contrast to Oak are two representatives of selfish passion: Troy, the romantic, fascinating trivialist, who has yet in him something not altogether ignoble; and the sombre, violent Boldwood, brooding, introspective, uncontrolled. These men are variants of the type that includes, with important individual differences, Wildeve in *The Return of the Native* and Fitzpiers in *The Woodlanders*. Bathsheba Everdene is the best representative of Hardy's belief in a woman's inability to press steadily and independently towards the goal that she has set before her. Despite herself, Bathsheba, with all her determination to manage her estate for herself, is dependent upon Oak, and though impatient of minor conventions she is sobered and rendered discreet by calamity in the perhaps too brief space of a few months. As a foil to her there is Troy's sweetheart Fanny, but the contrast is not so fully developed as is done in the case of the juxtaposed women in the two novels that have so much in common with *Far from the Madding Crowd*. The story is really of the loves of three men of widely contrasting temperament for one woman. One should note that the apparently gay title veils as deep meaning as did the light name of the preceding book. " Along the cool, sequestered vale of life " as passionate natures may be encountered, as high tragedies may be enacted as upon the highroads of the world.

This book established Hardy's place among the foremost living novelists. Indeed a contemporary reviewer declared that certain characteristics of the book secured him "a high place among novelists of any age." He did not have to undergo any such disheartening experience as Meredith's of a laborious climb to recognition not attained until his last years. As a partial offset to this good fortune his popularity entailed some lowering of his imagination's ideals to meet the demands of a great body of magazine readers. ᴜᴜᴜᴜᴜᴜᴜᴜᴜ

COMMENT has frequently been made upon the apparent fluctuations in Hardy's genius, which, instead of developing steadily from apprentice-work to masterpiece and thence to another masterpiece, has produced between novels of great strength and profundity other stories that already the world would be forgetting but for their connection with the five or six books of acknowledged excellence. This ebb and flow is due to the need of replenishment and refreshment after the severe intellectual and spiritual strain demanded by the major novels, after each of which (with one exception) come several fallow years. To gain renewed strength by turning to other and lighter themes is a wiser course than to exhaust fecundity in the first rush of genius as Dickens so nearly did.

The Hand of Ethelberta was published in 1876. It has been suggested that the, to us, almost incomprehensible strictures that were passed at the time upon Hardy's studies of rustic life (concerning which more will be said in a later chapter) may have suggested the sudden change of subject-matter. Hardy appears here to be venturing into the domain of George Meredith, just as Meredith, in *Rhoda Fleming,* grapples with a subject better suited to the genius of Hardy. Meredith might have done well with the theme of a low-born girl's attempt to establish herself

in the situation thrust upon her by a marriage into
"high life" followed swiftly by premature and almost penniless widowhood, and in so doing to found
the fortunes of her father and his large family. But
it did not suit Hardy. Some of the scenes are rather
lively and the portraits of the resourceful heroine's
sister and brother are attractive; but the high-born
lords and ladies are quite wooden and are not convincing even as rough sketches seen from the point of
view of the servants' hall. The story begins amusingly
enough; but it soon drags and as a whole it is quite
insignificant.

THE novel which in the opinion of many critics is
Hardy's most nearly perfect work of art as well as
his most profound and least biassed study of human
nature is *The Return of the Native*. This was published in 1878. Notwithstanding its admirable qualities it was not so well received as some of its forerun-
ners, one reviewer even pronouncing it "distinctly
inferior to anything of his which we have yet read."
The situation presented is that of *Far from the Madding Crowd* with certain variations: a love-entangle-
ment between three men and two women. Two of
these persons — Eustacia and Wildeve — are highly
complex natures, impulsive, passionate, selfish, but
not without some qualities that in other circumstances might have been turned to good; two others
— Thomasin and Venn — are steady, simple, and
courageous. The first two are at odds with life and in

violent war with the conditions among which they are placed; the second pair are steeped in, and in harmony with, their environment. One may well question the grim note which Hardy, in the definitive edition of the book, appended to it, to the effect that only the exigencies of periodical publication caused him to arrange an ending with the marriage of the two children of the heath and requesting readers of " an austere artistic code " to imagine that Thomasin remained a widow and that Venn disappeared from the country-side. A protest against the conventional " happy ending " was needed at the time and would have been wholesome. But to have ended this particular story in such a manner would have eliminated the *catharsis*, the cleansing of the passions, which is part of the function of tragedy. As the book stands, the implied lesson is effectively brought home by the destruction of the two rebels against circumstance in contrast to the serene content awarded those who submitted themselves to circumstance. There is a greater emphasis than heretofore upon the power of environment over the fortunes of humanity. The novelist develops with full and confident strength the line of thought somewhat crudely adumbrated in *A Pair of Blue Eyes*, for the tale is a tragedy of the human will, believing itself free yet ceaselessly entangled and thwarted by external forces. Egdon is the type of that Power that moves the world, a Power which is not inimical (for hostility implies intention, and intention consciousness) but indifferent to man. In some later novels and in many poems Hardy tends to differentiate more completely between Nature — that is, the natural world — and the Will of Force which governs it as well as man. All phenomena come to be looked upon as fellow-sufferers with man under a conscienceless and implacable despotism.

Clym Yeobright, "the Native," though entangled in the meshes that drag Eustacia and Wildeve to destruction, stands in a different relation to his environment from that of the two rebels and of Venn and Thomasin. Education has guided his aspirations to a height above his opportunities. Yet experience of the outer world, far from alienating him from the surroundings in which he has been brought up, has intensified his love of the heath. He is Hardy's most careful study of what he conceives to be the modern man, worn and saddened by thought. He is one who holds "the view of life as a thing to be put up with, replacing that zest for existence which was so intense in early civilizations." For "old-fashioned revelling in the general situation grows less and less possible as we uncover the defects of natural laws and see the quandary that man is in by their operation." (In such remarks as these we see Hardy feeling his way cautiously towards an explicit statement of the view of life inherent and implicit in the novels.) Yet Clym, too, when his aspirations become subdued to the possibilities of his position, is not, one imagines, positively unhappy; doubtless his work as an itinerant preacher brought him a fair degree of content.

Thomas Hardy

In Eustacia there is the conflict between stern, limited actualities and romantic imaginings. She is a more passionate Emma Bovary, far removed from the sordidness of a provincial French town, yet looking towards the vulgarities of Paris for the romance to which she is blind in the great heath around her; satisfying (like Emma), or attempting to satisfy, this craving for romance in a commonplace amour.

The Return of the Native reveals a deep and most moving love of the natural world, founded on the surest knowledge. The famous prelude-like opening is one of the most magnificent pieces of modern prose, reaching a level to which Hardy but seldom attains. The description of the heath enfolded by the night gradually resolves itself into the human business of the story. And throughout the book, ever and anon, a curtain seems to lift behind the actors, and we catch glimpses of the heath, impassive and enduring amid the tragedy that is so intense for the actors therein and yet is so light when set in the balance against natural forces.

ⅎⅎⅎⅎⅎⅎⅎ

AFTER the concentration required in the creation of this great romance refreshment was found in writing several books of slighter build. The first of these is *The Trumpet-Major,* published in 1880. This tale is to be associated with *Under the Greenwood Tree* as a study of feminine indecision between two lovers, set against a background of rustic life. As a whole it has been very variously estimated. A temporarily enfeebled imagination is exhibited by the presence of several " stock " literary types: the *miles gloriosus,* the miser, the faithful soldier and the fickle sailor. These last two remind one of the " faithful friends " or " two noble kinsmen " of so much earlier literature. The story is the first large sign of Hardy's interest in the period of the Napoleonic Wars; he has himself said that it was the consciousness that he had here barely touched the fringes of the great theme that kept him continually pondering upon it till at length it found full expression in *The Dynasts.* (The earliest notes for the epic-drama, it may be said here, date from the later seventies.) *The Trumpet-Major* is a remarkable resurrection of the life of a bygone time of crisis; the atmosphere of the village and of the old mill, the tranquil setting against the background of war are accomplished with a pleasing, quiet art. Hardy here gives freer rein than usual to imagery, to description for its own sake, to racy dialogue that has little bearing upon the action. As a whole his books lack the quality of gusto; that quality is certainly present here. The story is too protracted, but it leaves a pleasant taste in the mouth, and in tone it is the sweetest and serenest of all the novels.

The feminine flux of fancy portrayed in this book becomes the chief motive of *A Laodicean* (1881), by all odds the weakest of Hardy's books but in the consideration of which criticism is handicapped by the author's statement that it was in large part composed during convalescence from severe illness. The reappearance of a whole group of architects (absent from the novels since *A Pair of Blue Eyes*), with lengthy disquisitions upon the problems involved in the restoration of old buildings, together with a return to something of the technique of *Desperate Remedies*, points to a continued abeyance of the imaginative powers. The opening scene of the baptism, presenting, in a fashion better than any detailed description could have done, the vacillating heroine, is excellently done and was probably written before the illness that forced the author to fulfil as best he might the contract for serial publication to which he had agreed. The involved love-story is not worth untangling. De Stancy is a conventional figure, and his revolting bastard is of a type associated with the " Gothic " novel. The only noteworthy motive in the book, apart from that of feminine indeterminateness, is the influx of modern ideas and methods into Wessex; Paula, the heroine, comes of new commercial stock, but she lives in an old castle that embodies or symbolizes the dignity and romance and memories — and discomforts — of past times.

A third slight and in some respects rather tiresome story, *Two on a Tower* (1882), is notable for the manner in which the human emotions are projected against a background of infinite space, for the young hero is an astronomer; and a " stellar gauge " is thus afforded whereby may be measured the infinitesimal insignificance of the actions and emotions of such apparent importance to the actors themselves.

The function of Egdon Heath in an earlier novel is thus assumed here by the starry universe. The suggestion that it is a malign fatalism that conducts human affairs, just hinted at in previous books, is here marked; after *Two on a Tower* this idea, a relic of the anthropomorphic notions of Hardy's boyhood, yields place to a strict determinism.

The theme of an older woman's beautiful, unselfish, and half-maternal devotion to a young lover is suggestive of Balzac, who would have developed it, perhaps with greater profundity and certainly with more elaboration but hardly with greater delicacy and certainly with less charm. In some characters of earlier novels, especially in his portrait of Bathsheba Everdene, Hardy had indicated his sympathy with those who rebel against the lesser social conventions. Here this sympathy becomes outspoken and there appear definite attacks upon the restraint imposed by society upon the individual in a manner that points forward to *Tess* and *Jude*. These attacks inspired what Meredith in another connection once called " the low growls of British prudery." The grounds for unfavourable comment were what seemed to Victorian minds an over-frankness in the portrayal of sexual emotion and sexual relations, an apparent attack upon the sanctity of marriage, and a supposedly satiric intent in the portrait of the Bishop of Melchester. But there is no fighting quality in the book, no defiant hostility to society. The outlook upon life is tenderly meditative and melancholy. It lacks force.

And there is a detachment from life that seems to envelop the actors in the story in a sort of nebulous haze, as though events were seen through gauze curtains, that suggests the manner of Pater in the *Imaginary Portraits.*

For four years now Hardy published nothing except an article on "The Dorsetshire Labourer" (1883) to which reference will be made in a later chapter, and the pretty but fantastic and unimportant *Romantic Adventures of a Milkmaid* (also 1883), a mere novelette which may be dismissed with two remarks. The milkmaid's lover is a lime-burner; he recalls Venn, the reddleman, in the way in which his personality has been subdued to what he works in. The landscape is evidently a preliminary study for the elaborately wrought representations of similar country-side in the middle part of *Tess.* . . . These fallow years were also in part occupied with the pleasant task of designing and building Max Gate, the house on the outskirts of Dorchester to which the Hardys moved in 1885. Then came *The Mayor of Casterbridge* (1886), an astonishing rebirth of power in thought and art.

Interest in this book is not divided over a group of four or five people all portrayed with about the same amount of detail, but is concentrated in a manner that anticipates the technique of *Tess* and *Jude* upon a single man who represents, as Jude was later to represent still more harshly, the conflict of reason and impulse. The tragedy of Henchard's life does not lie in combinations of external circumstances, though they play their part. His environment casts no such blight upon his hopes as did Eustacia's upon hers. He carries his fate with him and had opposition arisen it would have worked itself out in much the same manner elsewhere as in Casterbridge. Character is Fate. Henchard's shrewd, proud, illiterate, forceful, generous, passionate nature dashes itself to pieces against its own qualities. To the lines in *Lear* which Hardy cites in the preface to *Tess*:

> As flies to wanton boys, are we to the gods,
> They kill us for their sport —

the clear-sightedness of Henchard and his humility would have compelled the reply, from the same tragedy:

> The gods are just, and of our pleasant vices
> Make instruments to plague us.

For the outcome is as inevitable as if it had been Egdon Heath that he dashed himself against. Fortune does not favour him; but the directing Force of the universe uses his own pride and high temper and stubbornness to work his ruin, notwithstanding his many splendid qualities of heart and head. This conception reaches to the very heart of tragedy, and the belated humility of his last visit to his foster-daughter renders the tragedy more poignant still. The other characters are less strongly imagined, and intentionally so in order to throw the picture of Henchard into high relief. The first Mrs. Henchard is a frail, pitiful shadow. Elizabeth-Jane, the sport of contending forces, wins happiness in the end through no effort of her own but as it were through the caprice of chance that awards indifferently caresses and blows to humanity. Lucetta is quite conventional and theatrical, a sort of dejected Mariana awaiting in her grange in the Channel Islands the return of another than Angelo, and later behaving as Hardy's fickle women are wont to behave. Farfrae, Henchard's Scotch steward and presently his rival, is unconvincingly drawn. Hardy knows his Southron; he does not know the Scot. But the idea behind the conception of Farfrae is an important one and connects *The Mayor of Casterbridge* with *A Laodicean*. When Farfrae takes charge of Henchard's business he introduces new and revolutionary methods into the conduct of affairs. As one of the townsmen remarks:

" ' Twas verily Fortune sent him to Henchard. His accounts were like a bramblewood when Mr. Farfrae came. He used to reckon his sacks by chalk strokes all in a row like garden-palings, measure his ricks by stretching with his arms, weigh his trusses by a lift, judge his hay by a chaw, and settle the price with a curse. But now this young, accomplished man does it all by ciphering and mensuration."

In his Northern canniness and energy and accuracy, contrasting with the easy-going, tradition-ridden, unambitious ways of the Southern folk, he thus typifies the ingress of new methods and ideas into Wessex. With him the Modern comes and before him the Immemorial has to yield.

The wife-selling episode with which the book opens is, it may be objected, too remote from ordinary experience (though analogous incidents have actually occurred) to afford a secure foundation for the story. But that objection once granted, in the impression that the novel makes of logical development, reserved strength, remorseless logic, artistic restraint, and control of materials there are found strong claims for regarding it as Hardy's most artistic achievement. One should mark such matters as the intimate but never obtrusive picture of the people and customs of the market-town; the subtle distinctions of shading to indicate the relative importance of the principal characters; the gradual decline of Henchard's fortunes, arrested for a moment with an irony that makes the outcome all the more bitter; the impression given of inevitability, as in that fine use of tragic anticipation when it is quietly announced that the years of Henchard's self-denying ordinance against liquor are almost up. It would be difficult to find an incident that is out of place or that has not its share in the outcome. The whole is thoroughly thought out and finely composed. What it lacks is charm, sweetness, poetry.

Two of these qualities, and something of bittersweetness as well, are present in the next novel, the most tender of all Hardy's books. The two phases of

Thomas Hardy

Hardy's period of master-craftsmanship overlap, for *The Mayor of Casterbridge* was quickly followed by a book that one is tempted to believe preceded it in conception, if not in composition. *The Woodlanders* (1887) belongs in theme with *Far from the Madding Crowd* and, even more closely, with *The Return of the Native*. For a third time we are presented with two contrasting pairs of men and women: Fitzpiers and Mrs. Charmond, Giles Winterborne and Marty South. Fitzpiers, the sensualist, has in him a certain intellectual quality that raises him a stage above the position of Troy and Wildeve and accounts in part for the mercifulness of Hardy in leaving it at least an open question whether the experiences that he has undergone may not make his later life a not altogether useless one. Felice Charmond is less elaborately portrayed than Eustacia Vye, less romantic, more worldly, more hardened, even more misplaced in the forest than is Eustacia on the heath. Giles and Marty are the counterparts of Venn and Thomasin with this difference, that whereas in the earlier story the tragedy in which the heath-dwellers are involved leaves them scarred but whole, the woodlanders are destroyed by the capricious destiny that spares the two principal causes of their ruin. Apart from these four people, yet intertwined in fortune with them, is Grace Melbury, a female counterpart of Clym Yeobright. Like Clym she has been raised by education above her surroundings; like him this involves her in tragedy; like him, though with characteristic feminine indecision, she becomes subdued again to her native environment; unlike him, and like a woman, she turns back to the outer world. It is left to the chorus of rustics to speculate upon her possible chances of happiness elsewhere. Apart from its transcendent interest as a story, the significance of the book lies in the exquisitely observed and minutely recorded woodland scenes and customs, in the sense now clearly implied that Nature and man are fellow-sufferers from the burden of life, in the overflowing sympathy apparent beneath the reticence of the account of Giles's death, in the pathetic figure of Marty South, and in the fact that here for the last time the novelist's "objectivity" is retained and his personal opinions kept austerely unexpressed.

ᒐᒐᒐᒐ

FOR several years past, ever since 1879, Hardy had been publishing short stories from time to time. Some of these were now collected in the volume called *Wessex Tales* (1888), which was followed by three other similar collections: *A Group of Noble Dames* (1890), *Life's Little Ironies* (1894), and *A Changed Man* (1913). In the definitive Wessex edition of Hardy's works there has been some rearrangement of these tales. Disregarding chronology for the moment, one may consider these four volumes together before going on to the last three novels.

In its employment of the marvellous and the fantastic *Wessex Tales* harks back to Hardy's earlier

years and is in striking contrast to *Life's Little Ironies.*
Three stories are particularly memorable in this first
set. These are " The Three Strangers," " The Withered
Arm," and " The Distracted Preacher." The first two
of these, and several others in the book, are studies in
the freaks of coincidence. The well-known tale of
" The Three Strangers," which has been successfully
dramatized, narrates the extraordinary chance meeting of a hangman and his intended victim and the victim's brother at a shepherd's hut. It may well be taken
as a model of what the short story should be. The setting is clear-cut, picturesque, and in ironical contrast
to the circumstance of the meeting; the situation is
deftly and rapidly outlined; the episode proceeds
swiftly to a sensational but logical climax, and then
the stormy night shuts out the scene. The suppressed
terror of the escaped thief; the unconscious cheerfulness and professional pride of the hangman; the
dumbfounded distress of the thief's brother — all are
placed ironically against the background of the shepherd's Christening feast. (W. H. Hudson's readers
should compare this tale with his story "The Old
Thorn " which tells of an execution for sheep-
stealing.) " The Withered Arm " tells of the chance
simultaneous occurrence of a dreadful dream or
hallucination of an incubus and of the beginning of
a terrible disease. The coincidence is so tremendous
that, though it can be accounted for rationally, it
almost forces the acceptance of a supernatural explanation. It shows the degree to which the power to

suggest mystery and dread may take the place, in a rationalistic age, of the downright supernaturalism of an age of romance. Here the various elements of the tale — the vengeful spirit of the cast-off mistress who has turned witch, the deformity of the bride and her gradual alienation from her husband, the dreadful counsel offered her by the conjuror, and the husband's growing, wistful remorse at his abandonment of his bastard son — are kept well apart until they are suddenly brought together in the overwhelming climax at the hangman's cottage. " The Distracted Preacher " is the product of a very different mood. It is a delightfully humorous story, the irony for once being put to the service of laughter. The setting reminds one of the opening pages of Conrad and Hueffer's *Romance.* For the story is of a conscientious young preacher who becomes enamoured of a fascinating young widow engaged in the trade of smuggling liquor from France. Love leads his moral sense far astray, but he has his revenge, for in later years, when he has won her for his wife, the one-time smuggler writes edifying tracts against the shady occupation in which she had formerly been so expert. Here, as in *The Trumpet-Major,* Hardy makes use of material derived in very large part from the actual past of his country-side.

Such material is again employed in *A Group of Noble Dames,* a second collection of brief narratives published serially in 1890 and in enlarged form in 1891. Nowhere else in his fiction, save in *The*

Trumpet-Major, does Hardy rely to such an extent upon country records and current local traditions. The tales, as the title indicates, concern the fortunes and misfortunes of various great ladies of Wessex. They are, as one would expect, a series of studies of feminine psychology, of women acting in immediate obedience to emotional impulse. All centre in marital difficulties and entanglements. The first few end happily enough (the first of all romantically so); but as the book progresses the tone of the stories becomes more and more sombre and the last are tragic indeed. Unfortunately Hardy's tendency to extravagance is manifest to a degree that carries some of the tales (notably that of Barbara) to a pitch of melodramatic absurdity that is a cause of distress to his judicious admirers. The stories are held together by a very charming variety of the "frame-tale," a device of long literary ancestry which had never become obsolete, as Mrs. Gaskell's *Round the Sofa* can witness, and which has of late been used in Maurice Hewlett's *New Canterbury Tales.* The Casterbridge antiquarian club is prevented from taking its annual walking-tour by a heavy storm, and to beguile the rainy afternoon and evening one member after another relates a story of the neighbourhood. The various narrators are not particularly individualized nor is there any obvious attempt to suit the several stories to their tellers. The touch is light and there is no pretence of psychological profundity or any effort to present a comprehensive view of life such as is found in the *Decameron* and in

Chaucer. But, following these great models, there are brief interpolated discussions by the members of the club; and the change in the character of the tales as the afternoon wears on suggests a successful imitation of Boccaccio.

Another and even simpler form of the " frame-tale " is used in the series of colloquial sketches entitled " A Few Crusted Characters " in *Life's Little Ironies*. These sketches form a little masterpiece of " regional " literature. In grace, delicacy, humour, felicity of setting, and knowledge of the folk-background they recall *Under the Greenwood Tree*. People who associate Hardy overmuch with gloom should turn to these tales.

The stories contained in *Life's Little Ironies* were written between 1889 and 1893. They are of a more philosophical cast than are the earlier short tales. Most of them are further illustrations of the point of view set forth in *The Mayor of Casterbridge,* that " Character is Fate." The " irony " comes generally from no fortuitous combination of external events but from the inherent qualities of the protagonist. It shows the perversion of men's purposes and the destruction of their happiness by circumstance working through some innate weakness in the character of the individual upon whom the interest is centered or through the prejudices and timidity of some one else which block his plans and hinder him from setting to rights the little world in which he moves. " On the Western Circuit " and " For Conscience's Sake " illustrate this. In the very powerful tale of "A Tragedy of Two Ambitions" the terrible theme resembles Gwendolen's refusal to throw a rope to the drowning Grandcourt in *Daniel Deronda*. This story of the two ambitious curates whose aspirations are thwarted by their drunken father is masterly. The technique of these stories is everywhere about the same: the protagonist is set in the midst of a situation outlined with swift, deft strokes; this situation works up rapidly to a climax; there is a crash, followed by a new adjustment of the component parts of the original situation. The bitterly ironic tone of almost all the tales connects this volume with the series of "Satires of Circumstance" in verse, published twenty years afterwards.

There is no such unity of tone in the miscellany called *A Changed Man* which contains little of importance. The tale which gives the general title to the book, like several others therein, is in a general way like the stories in *Life's Little Ironies* but less meritorious than they. "A Tryst at an Ancient Earthwork" is noteworthy as being almost the only place in his writings where Hardy has made imaginative use of the gigantic ancient fortress, Maiden Castle. "Alicia's Diary" differs from all his other stories, except his first juvenile experiment, in being written, as the title indicates, in the first person. But the book as a whole must be regarded merely as a gathering together of the by-products of a great career.

These four series of short stories best show the

side of Hardy's genius that has been content to leave unexpressed the implications that reside in the arrangement of human affairs that he sets forth. There is no room for expansion, no opportunity for explicit comment. The artistic unity thus achieved is often of a high order. But there is loss as well as gain.

ᴜᴜᴜᴜᴜᴜᴜᴜᴜ

THE first notes for *Jude the Obscure* were jotted down in 1887, and it cannot have been much later that Hardy began the composition of *Tess of the D'Urbervilles*. That he set about the writing of these books with a full consciousness that they would occasion adverse comment and disturb many minds is shown by the fact that before *Tess* appeared he published two articles that are in the nature of manifestos. These are: "The Profitable Reading of Fiction," published in *The Forum* (New York) in 1888; and "Candour in English Fiction," which appeared in *The New Review* in 1890, the latter being part of a discussion to which Sir Walter Besant and Mrs. Lynn Linton also contributed articles. The greater part of Hardy's earlier essay is taken up with matters to which attention will be devoted in the next chapter; but two sentences quite evidently prepare the way for *Tess*:

It is unfortunately quite possible to read the most elevating works of imagination in our own or any language, and, by fixing the regard on the wrong side of the subject, to gather not a grain of wisdom from them, nay,

sometimes positive harm. What author has not had his
experience of such readers? — the mentally and morally
warped one of both sexes, who will, where practicable, so
twist plain and obvious meanings as to see in an honest
picture of human nature an attack on religion, morals, or
institutions.

The later article is so direct as to make it certain that
Hardy had in mind, in speaking so plainly, the novel
he was about to send forth. He pleads for sincerity;
the writer of fiction should have liberty to express
candidly the same opinions that are expressed everywhere in society. He should be allowed to give full
weight to the passions. It should be recognized that
some novelists write not for school-girls or for the
circulating libraries but for adult thoughtful men
and women. Within his sphere should be permitted
to come mature and balanced consideration of such
matters especially as the relation of man to woman,
as the position of man in the universe, and as the
problems of religious beliefs. Hardy is here evidently
giving vent to his indignation against those conventions of serial publication that necessitated the bowd-
lerization of several of his novels when they appeared
in the first magazine version. (In the first published
form of *Tess*, for example, the hoary device of a
mock marriage took the place of the seduction to
which, in the final version, Tess herself assents.)
Equally obviously, he is contrasting his own purposes
and ideals with those of, say, Sir Walter Besant and
other writers of novels which, as the French book-

lists have it, *" peuvent être mis entre toutes les mains."*

Tess of the D'Urbervilles, the most widely read of all his books, was published in complete form (save for a passage accidentally overlooked at the time and not incorporated in the novel till 1912) in November, 1891, several parts of the book having previously appeared in magazines. A tale of calamity as old as human nature, or at any rate as old as social conventions, is told with tender and sympathetic sincerity. Hardy here follows in the footsteps of the various Victorians who with greater or less tact and assurance have told of seduction: one has in mind especially Dickens, George Eliot, Mrs. Gaskell, and Meredith. *Esther Waters,* the finest of all English novels on this theme, belongs to another and more modern school.

Of one of his former books a critic of the time had remarked that Hardy " like a true artist, never attempts by any indication of his own preferences to bias his reader's judgment." In *Tess* Hardy abandons his " objectivity." He forsakes his impassivity; he has a thesis to propound, and he does so in a recriminating fashion. This is not to say that to employ the novel as a means of promulgating a writer's views is necessarily and inherently wrong. But in so doing Hardy left behind him one of the characteristics of the earlier Wessex novels that was most impressive. The point of his development in lengthy fiction is reached where he is emerging from the implicit to the explicit in the illustration and exposition of his view of life. This change may well have been prompted by the reception of former romances by a public that greeted him as a capital story-teller while refusing to recognize the substratum of philosophic implication. The explanation suggests a comparison with Meredith's development in the face of public indifference; and the later phases of Henry James's career also come to mind. Therefore, though, as has just been said, *Tess* is Hardy's most widely known book, neither it nor *Jude* is really thoroughly characteristic. The mysterious light which, like that which appears ever and anon in *The Dynasts,* is shed over the action of *The Return of the Native* or of *The Woodlanders,* giving an effect approximating that of the supernatural, has almost disappeared. Hardy is more modern, more didactic, more realistic, less a part of the half-pagan primitive peasantry among whom he grew up — in a word, less Hardy.

It is possible, by setting certain passages in *Tess* over against certain others, to involve Hardy in a maze of self-contradictions. Nature is depicted at times as cruel and without sympathy; yet there are repeated suggestions of advocacy of the free play of natural impulses. The very measures that have been taken for the protection of society against the mercilessness of Nature are harshly attacked. And this attack is in itself an admission (which Hardy has elsewhere indicated as the centre of his practical philosophy) that man can ameliorate the conditions in which he lives. Yet man is not a free agent. It is possible so to follow Tess's career — and in fact the *Spectator's* reviewer at the time did so — as to make her out very largely the victim of her own stupidity and needless timidity. But these very qualities are part of her nature and beyond her control. Other critics have denounced the execution of Tess as an impossible extravagance. This, however, is to forget the severity of the penal code as it existed of recent years in England; one may compare the exaction of death for sheep-stealing in " The Three Strangers." Other episodes can be picked out in which the writer seems to lose his self-control, the capital instance being the sketch of the vicar who refuses burial for Tess's baby in consecrated ground. In general an effect of incoherence is produced by the indiscriminate blows rained now upon ephemeral remediable wrongs, now upon the very nature of things.

And yet, when all is said, the impression that *Tess* leaves upon almost every candid and clearsighted reader is one of power and insight and sympathy and beauty — and hopefulness. The conclusion we are asked to draw is that passivity, quietism, is the only remedy for the ills of human life. But we do nothing of the sort. We deny that the book presents any general indictment of life. For these evils are not inherent in the nature of things. They are open to cure. Already, in the three decades that have passed since *Tess* appeared, sentiment has made some progress. And the world is not altogether wrong that has in it such a place as Talbothay's dairy, and a woman of such native loveliness of character as Tess, and, indeed, a man of such qualities as he who tells her story. If at times the presentation of some episodes is not convincing, the presentation of other episodes is profoundly so. It is difficult to accept as in keeping with Tess's character the first sojourn with Alec following the night in the Chase. In spite of his emphasis upon her innocent and unsuspecting adolescence, Hardy fails to give a convincing analysis of the motives and impulses that drew her to Alec. But note, as one of the many offsets to this, the exquisite art with which the passionate love of the dairy-maids for Angel Clare is kept from slipping over either into the maudlin on one side or the farcical on the other. The character-drawing is generally of a high order, the chief exceptions being the two brothers of Angel Clare and Tess's father and young sister. Alec D'Urberville is portrayed in really masterly fashion. He is the arch-sensualist of the novels, without Troy's remorse, or Fitzpiers's intellectuality, or Wildeve's courageous last moments. The subtle way in which his conversion is ascribed to a slight shift of point of view under the influence of the same sensual temperament, is perhaps Hardy's finest achievement in psychological analysis, however much of suggestion it may owe to a passage in *Madame Bovary:*

It was less a reform than a transfiguration. The former curves of sensuousness were now modulated to lines of devotional passion. The lip-shapes that had meant seductiveness were now made to express supplication; the

glow on the cheek that yesterday could be translated as
riotousness was evangelized to-day into the splendour of
pious rhetoric; animalism had become fanaticim; Pagan-
ism Paulinism; the bold rolling eye that had flashed upon
her form in the old time with such mastery now beamed
with the rude energy of a theolatry that was almost
ferocious.

Equally subtle — and a more difficult task — is the
delineation of Angel Clare. His nearest analogue in
the novels is, of course, Knight in *A Pair of Blue Eyes,*
but he belongs with all those men who have partially
shaken off the tyranny of convention and yet, while
fancying themselves intellectually free, are bound
faster than they realize by the conventions which
they pride themselves upon having put by. The
much-criticized episode of Clare's suggestion to Izz
to accompany him to Brazil is in reality thoroughly
in character. The suggestion comes in a moment of
revolt against those conventions, obedience to which
has ruined his life. It is sudden, not reasoned; and it
is checked in a moment by the return of thought. His
is a limed soul that, struggling to be free, is but the
more engaged. He is thus portrayed and the function
of admiration or condemnation is left to the critics,
who have accordingly divided, Mr. Abercrombie, for
example, repudiating him utterly, while Mr. Duffin
writes of " the celestial beauty " of his character. If,
bearing in mind that he refused to extend to Tess the
very forgiveness that he asked of her and received —
Knight at least exacted of Elfrida only what he was

ready and able to offer her — one is inclined to exclaim of Clare, *Guarda e passa!* it must be remembered that Hardy himself does not pass judgement on him.

Of the other characters it is not necessary to speak here; something will be said later of the elder Mr. Clare. Nor is it necessary to comment in detail upon the very beautiful descriptions of Nature, the Wessex background, particularly of the Chase, of the life on the great dairy-farms, and of Stonehenge. In some of the earlier books place and season had been to some extent fitted into accord with the action of the story. In *Tess* this adjustment is managed with the highest art. But consideration of this matter also is postponed for the present. When all these merits of character-drawing and nature-description and artistic construction have been recognized, the final appeal of the novel is nevertheless not one to our aesthetic sense but to our emotions. The memory of *Tess* that abides, one dares say, in the mind of nearly every reader, is of Hardy's tenderness.

Along with the great popular success of *Tess* (which was reinforced when it was promptly turned into a play) went, as is still well remembered, a clamour from those whom prudery or conventionality or timidity rendered unfit to comprehend its purpose. In an addition to the original preface Hardy divulged his sensitiveness to these criticisms. Another and more natural accompaniment of its success was the appearance of two critical studies of Hardy's works: Lionel Johnson's *The Art of Thomas Hardy* (1894; reissued 1922) and Annie Macdonell's *Thomas Hardy* (1895). The former book, now long out of print, is a carefully wrought, elaborate, Pater-esque, perhaps over " literary " monograph by a man of delicate sensibilities, whose catholic sympathies in literature enable him to rise above the fundamental philosophic differences that divide him from Hardy. The latter book is an unpretentious and popular pre-sentation of certain phases of Hardy's work. It is noteworthy that so late as 1895 Miss Macdonell could summarize Hardy's claims to recognition as "story-teller, picture-maker, humorist," directly denying him any special gifts as poet or thinker. It was just this reputation that for so long retarded the compre-hension of his thought and that prepared the way for the outcry raised by *Jude the Obscure*.

ⅬⅬⅬⅬⅬⅬⅬⅬⅬ

THE WELL-BELOVED, originally called *The Pursuit of the Well-Beloved*, appeared serially in 1892 though it was not put into book-form until 1897. It marks another of those periods of re-creation that we have observed several times before. The theme is Shelleyan:

> In many mortal forms I rashly sought
> The shadow of that idol of my thought.

The possibilities of this theme had been suggested in the character of Fitzpiers in *The Woodlanders*.

Thomas Hardy

" Human love," says Fitzpiers, " is a subjective thing.
. . . It is joy accompanied by an idea which we
project against any suitable object." And again, at
the first sight of Grace, his thought takes this turn:
" Nature has at last recovered her lost union with
the Idea." In more than one poem Hardy recurs to
this subject, particularly in that phase of the experience when the light of the Idea is vanishing
from the face and form which it had previously
illumined and which is then found to be as commonplace as any other. In *The Well-Beloved* this
theme, which lies beneath the tale of Fitzpiers's flit-
tings from Grace to Sue and to Mrs. Charmond,
and to who knows whom in later unrecounted
phases of his history, is worked out in ingenious but,
before the end, wearisome detail in the story of
Jocelyn Pierston, as he pursues *la figlia della sua
mente, l'amorosa idea,* the only true well-beloved,
from momentary incarnation to incarnation, as it
lends its divine light now to some woman of society,
now to a peasant girl, and as it dwells more persist-
ently in the persons of the three Avices — grand-
mother, mother, and child — whom the disciple of
the *Vita Nuova* and *Epipsychidion* has loved in
youth, in manhood, and in old age. The conception
of Pierston as a sculptor has meaning in it, for his art
is only another phase of the same pursuit. The mention of the *Vita Nuova* suggests perhaps a false
analogy, for in Dante's experience love has been
roused by the image of perfection and can never for-

sake its object; in Pierston's life it is roused again and again only by the hope, destined ever to disappointment, that perfection will be found in one or another of the succeeding objects of his desire. Shelley goes farther yet, for he loves the Idea which, as he is well aware, will quit each separate incarnation in turn. *The Well-Beloved* plays cleverly with a subtle theme, but it would have gained, not lost, had Hardy discarded the unconvincing attempt to account in part for Pierston's temperament by the peculiar and isolated environment of his youth. Nor does his marriage with a faded woman of the world, whom long since the Idea had temporarily transfigured in his imagination, help matters. Irony is out of accord with fantasy. But the fantasticality and dullness (in which the lack of any variety of interest plays a great part) must not blind the reader to the book's significance in the history of Hardy's development. In any later novel one must expect a substratum of allegory.

ᴜᴜᴜᴜᴜᴜᴜᴜᴜᴜ

JUDE THE OBSCURE was published in 1895, parts of it having already appeared serially under the title *Hearts Insurgent*. To attempt to appraise it is a difficult task. It has been ridiculed; it has been seriously controverted; it has been indulgently regarded as an unfortunate blunder on the part of a once-great artist; it has been called "one of the most illustrious things in literature." This much may be safely said, that the judgement of posterity upon it will be partly determined in accordance with whether the novelist's function is held to be the impartial and impassive reflection of life or whether he may take as his mission the promulgation of new and important ideas. By the old test, the test of "objectivity,"*Jude* fails to a degree greater even than does *Tess,* for though there are no such philosophic digressions as occur in *Tess,* the novelist is here even farther removed from austere self-control. By the other test it may be regarded as a milestone of advance, for it opens up new avenues of thought, it poses deliberately and courageously questions that all the world now faces. It caused a storm of protest on its appearance. Not the least insult that was heaped upon its writer was the classing of him with certain seekers after notoriety as a member of "the anti-marriage league" (the phrase is Mrs. Oliphant's). This hostility has persisted, and within the last few years a writer who claims to be a historian of the English novel has spoken of the "Hardy-Caine" school of fiction, a bracketing that needs no comment. The only permanent harm that the onslaught did was that, as Hardy definitely stated, the experience completely "cured" him of any further interest in novel-writing.

Structurally *Jude* belongs mid-way between *The Woodlanders* and *The Return of the Native* on the one hand, and *The Mayor of Casterbridge* and *Tess* on the other. Like the latter books, it concentrates attention upon one leading figure; yet, as in the former books, there is a complex situation arising out of the love-life of four closely allied people: two men and two women. A certain stiffening of the imagination is apparent in the repetition of situations from the earlier novels. This repetition is of another sort from that seen in *Tess* which reworks in a graver, more mature, more realistic way the leading motive of *A Pair of Blue Eyes*. In *Jude* the repetitions seem to be unconsciously done. The relationship of Jude and Phillotson is analogous to that of Smith and Knight. The grim story of Jude's forbears recalls the legend of the D'Urberville coach. Jude is reluctant to tell Sue of his connection with Arabella just as Tess makes repeated and half-hearted efforts to acquaint Clare with her history. Arabella turns up (by a coincidence that strains probability to the limit) at the crisis of Jude's fate as Alec does at the time of Tess's abandonment. Jude returns to Arabella as Tess had returned to Alec. In Tess herself there had been something of the precocious pessimism that is exaggerated in Jude's son to the point of caricature. The unity of place — certainly no *sine qua non* but magnificently adhered to in the novels of the middle years — is discarded more completely than in *Tess* and without the counterbalancing advantage there seen of harmonizing the event with the place in which it occurs.

There is far more matter in *Jude* than can possibly be condensed into a paragraph or two, more perhaps, as Hardy confesses, than the novelist consciously put there. But it is possible to indicate very briefly some of the lines of thought. The central theme is "the tragedy of unrealized aims." This has been the motive of many of the tales in *Life's Little Ironies*. Here we are presented with a man who is well-meaning and who holds a high ideal before him. But he comes of tainted stock, he is of low birth and narrow circumstances, and he is constantly being dragged down by his temperament. In the very hour of his visions of Christminster, the "City of Light," seen now in his dreams, now in reality far off at sunset, there rushes upon him an irresistible inclination towards women and presently he is entrapped into a sordid marriage. Jude experiences to the full "the fret and fever, derision and disaster, that may press in the wake of the strongest passion known to humanity"; and behind the temptation of sexual passion lurks another: the desire for strong liquor. Some hostile reviewers charged Hardy with putting to the credit of this man every aspiration, every fine yearning, and to the blame of circumstance each backsliding, each error, each yielding to desire. The charge misses the point of the whole tragedy: the book is not a denial of the existence of those happy souls who rise above temptations to the realizations of their ideals. It is the story of a man who (in Burns's most pathetic self-condemnatory words) is a "poor, damned, incautious, duped, unfortunate fool, the sport, the miserable victim of . . . hypochondriac imaginations, agonizing sensibility, and bedlam passions."

The wearisomely repeated attacks upon the permanency of the marriage bond are of secondary importance, for the handicap of an unwise union is merely the instrument of circumstance for thwarting Jude's aspiring desires. It must be noted, however, that these attacks are made more frequently by the characters in the book than by the author. In private conversation Hardy insisted that his opposition to marriage had been absurdly exaggerated and misunderstood. But the special prominence of the marital relation in this book can be connected closely with the philosophic systems of Schopenhauer and von Hartmann (of which something more must be said later.) As they watch a newly married couple Jude says to Sue:

" We are a little beforehand, that's all. In fifty, a hundred years the descendants of these two will act and feel worse than we. They will see weltering humanity still more vividly than we do now, as ' shapes like our own selves hideously multiplied,' and will be afraid to reproduce them."

Again the caution is needed that it is a character, not the author, *qui parle*. One is reminded, however, of Schopenhauer's famous and terrible indictment of lovers as " traitors to the race." For beneath the harsh realism of the story there is evidently allegory. The Will-Not-to-Exist is on the increase. The Intellect (which realizes the uselessness of life) is encroaching upon the domain of the Heart (which contains the instinct of reproduction.) In Jude, the male, the rational element is more highly developed, though it is ever and anon dragged down by the body. Arabella, on the other hand, is the very embodiment of Schopenhauer's view of woman as set forth in the famous essay. She is the mere instrument of the Will-to-Live. Sue is intended to represent the modern type of woman that is slowly emerging, one in whom the reason is asserting itself with a consequent approximation to the position of modern man. There is no half-allegorical implication in her final lapse; in returning to her husband she merely reenacts the inability to press on in a chosen independent direction which one expects in Hardy's women. Between the two women, between Reason and Instinct, as between the Good and Evil Angels of the old moralities, stands Jude. The atrocious little figure of " Father Time," his murder of Sue's babies and his own suicide, are prophecies of the future generations, foretold by von Hartmann, who will thus rid themselves of the burden of the mystery of the world. A fog of thought, perhaps one should say a miasma of despair, has settled down over the life depicted in this book. Through it the figures move dimly, sordidly, confusedly. The clear-cut outlines of earlier novels have disappeared.

Jude the Obscure is the only one of Hardy's books through which there gleams no hope at all. The curtain falls in *Far from the Madding Crowd* upon Oak and Bathsheba, less ardent, less joyous than before their bitter experiences, but content. At the end of *The Return of the Native* Venn's fidelity is rewarded and Clym finds comfort in his work as a lay missionary. *The Woodlanders* closes as Fitzpiers and Grace go from the scene with a chance at least of future happiness, while Marty South at the grave of Winterborne is a pathetic rather than a tragic figure. *The Mayor of Casterbridge* concludes with the deliberate statement of Elizabeth-Jane's " unbroken tranquillity " in adult life. We have already noted the hopefulness, put there consciously or not, in *Tess*. But in *Jude* there is no hope, no cleansing of the passions, no sense of " calm of mind, all passion spent." The darkness is utterly unrelieved; the humour of the earlier books is gone; no one is ever thoughtless or light-hearted. The words of Job which are upon Jude's dying lips seem not sufficiently despairing, for Job could say, " Though He slay me, yet will I trust in Him." Here we are brought to think rather of the grand chorus of the dead in Leopardi:

> In te, morte, si posa
> Nostra ignuda natura;
> Lieta no, ma sicura
> Dell' antico dolor. . . .
> Però ch' esser beato
> Nega ai mortali e nega a' morti il fato.

One cannot leave this great and terrible book without noting the power that has kept remorselessly to one theme, that has held the attention unswervingly upon one characer, that has refused to lighten the burden of the story by the factitious means of making that character, or indeed any person in the book, attractive, appealing, or anything but drab and commonplace, and that has carried through the whole story in monotone. In moments of cool analysis one may be tempted to ask whether it is not the author himself who has doomed his puppets to disaster, for there is little individuality in the several characters who are differentiated one from another by little save differences in opinion. But the unquestionably powerful impression made is an answer to that criticism. Almost the opening words describe Jude as " the sort of man who was born to ache a good deal before the fall of the curtain upon his unnecessary life should signify that all was well with him again." Here we have the final example in Hardy of the substitution of the instrument of tragic anticipation for the instrument of tragic suspense. The theme is announced immediately; and the heart-aches, the needlessness, the falling curtain, and the return to " dateless oblivion and divine repose " succeed each other like movements in a sombre symphony. Nor, finally, can one leave *Jude* without mention of the wonderful scene of his first evening in the " City of Light " when there throng around him memories of Christminster's illustrious dead and he seems to hear their voices, in diverse tones but all suggesting the way towards intellectual triumphs.

ᴜᴜᴜᴜᴜᴜᴜᴜ

His interest in creative romance failing him, Hardy turned again to poetry. The poetic gift, though hidden almost completely from the public, had not been allowed to rust in him unused through all these years. He now entered upon the second portion of his career and produced a body of verse of merits entirely independent of his work in fiction. This verse must ·be considered later in a separate chapter. For the sake of convenience, however, the present chapter may conclude with a brief account of his life since the publication of *The Well-Beloved,* the last novel to appear in book-form.

In 1898 *Wessex Poems* appeared with illustrations by the author. There followed in 1901 *Poems of the Past and the Present.* Before either of these collections was published Hardy had laid down, about 1897, the general plan and had begun the composition of the tremendous epic-drama of *The Dynasts* (three parts: 1903–6–8) which occupied most of his attention till its completion in September, 1907. He issued five more volumes of miscellaneous verse: *Time's Laughing-Stocks* (1909), *Satires of Circumstance* (1914), *Moments of Vision* (1917), *Late Lyrics and Earlier* (1922), and *Human Shows* (1925). In 1912 he supervised the publication of the Wessex edition of his writings in prose and verse, contributing to it a new general preface, additional prefaces to many of the novels, and a few notes. In this definitive edition the novels are arranged not chronologically but in accordance with a not altogether satisfactory scheme in three divisions as

Thomas Hardy

"Novels of Character and Environment," "Romances and Fantasies" and "Novels of Ingenuity."

In 1923 appeared *The Famous Tragedy of the Queen of Cornwall*, a stark, swift, dramatic rendering of the story of Tristram and Iseult. Hardy's attempt to reconcile the two conflicting versions of the death of the lovers is more ingenious than convincing; and though not without passion and intensity the play cannot be numbered among his important works.

The position of pre-eminence that Hardy held among living English writers after the death of Swinburne and Meredith has been recognized, though it has been a matter for regret to his admirers that his fame upon the Continent was insufficient to bring to him the Nobel Prize. After Meredith's death he succeeded him as President of the Society of British Authors. In 1910 the Order of Merit was bestowed upon him. In 1912 he received the Gold Medal of the Royal Society of Literature, an honour rarely given. A tribute of a different kind is the increasing number of critical studies of his writings that have appeared. Several recent ones supplement and in part supersede the earlier monographs by Lionel Johnson and Annie Macdonell. The most brilliant of these is by Lascelles Abercrombie (1912) who has the advantage of a poet's imaginative sympathy with a fellow-craftsman and who has achieved a book noteworthy for its architectonic skill. The most ambitious is F. A. Hedgcock's Sorbonne dissertation, *Thomas Hardy, Penseur et Artiste* (1910) which, inquiring

more deeply than does Mr. Abercrombie, brings the
sex-conflict that forms so large a part of Hardy's
subject-matter into proper relation with the philosophic doctrine of the struggle between Intellect and
Intuition. Unfortunately many pages of this bulky
book are occupied with mere summaries of the plots
of the novels. Moreover there are errors of attribu-
tion caused by the effort to discern realities under fic-
tional scenes and to make autobiographical facts out
of pure inventions. Besides other monographs and dis-
sertations, English and American, there are studies
by Harold Child and by H. C. Duffin (both 1916),
the former a brief but excellent summary, the latter
a larger and enthusiastic but rather ill-balanced piece
of work; *The Technique of Thomas Hardy* by J. W.
Beach (1922); *Thomas Hardy's Universe* by Ernest
Brennecke, Jr. (1924); a so-called *Life of Thomas
Hardy* (1925) by the same author; and — announced
as this book goes to press — a *Study* by Arthur Symons (1928). F. O. Saxelby has produced a *Thomas
Hardy Dictionary* of the names and places in all the
writings, a monument of patient industry. There is
a host of books about the Wessex country; a few only
need be mentioned here: C. G. Harper's *The Hardy
Country* (which has some excellent illustrations, including several of peasants at their work); B. C. A.
Windle's *The Wessex of Thomas Hardy* (which contains many pleasant line-drawings by E. H. New);
Sidney Heath's *The Heart of Wessex;* and, most
authoritative of all, Hermann Lea's *Thomas Hardy's*

Wessex which is issued as a supplementary volume to the Wessex edition of the works.

On November 27, 1912, Mrs. Thomas Hardy died. The group of " Poems of 1912–1913," destined, one hopes, to be known by the better title *Veteris vestigia flammae*, which Hardy wrote in her memory, are both touching and extraordinary, quite unlike any other elegies in the language. On her grave in Stinsford Church are the poignant words: " This for Remembrance." In 1914 Hardy married again, his second wife being Miss Florence Emily Dugdale, an old friend, who has been herself favourably known as a writer of books for children. During the Great War Hardy published a number of poems on public events as well as a letter to the *Times* on the bombardment of Rheims Cathedral. In 1920–21 the magnificent Mellstock edition of his works appeared. Late in that year there was unveiled at Dorchester a tablet to the memory of the townsmen who had fallen in the War. This was designed by Thomas Hardy and bears the following words from one of his poems as the motto:

None dubious of the cause, none murmuring.

Could better words have been found to inscribe above the names of those who fell in battle?

ururururururu

SHORTLY before the grand old poet's last illness his publishers, Messrs. Macmillan, reissued *The Dynasts* in a magnificent edition, worthy of its greatness.

The Novels

The etched portrait by Francis Dodd which serves as a frontispiece is so striking a likeness as to deserve special mention. The task of affixing his signature to each copy of this edition was probably the last work of the pen which had been active for so many years.

A chill caught about the middle of December 1927 developed into an alarming illness. There were fluctuations in his condition giving rise to alternate hopes and fears; but in the end the exhaustion of extreme age overtook him, and Hardy died in the arms of his wife on Wednesday evening, January 11, 1928. On Monday, January 16, his ashes were laid away in the Poets' Corner of Westminster Abbey. Statesmen, artists and men of letters with a vast number of men and women drawn together by their common admiration of the great poet gathered to do honour to his memory. The choir sang the *Nunc dimittis* and Newman's hymn; and the lesson read was that chapter from *Ecclesiasticus* which bids us all praise famous men and our fathers which were before us, whose bodies are buried in peace but whose name liveth forever more. At the same hour the heart of Thomas Hardy was buried in the graveyard of Stinsford Church, the Mellstock of the Wessex novels, a little way above Bockhampton Bridge, within sound of the murmur of the Froom.

3

Some Matters of Technique and Style

THE titles of some of the monographs upon Hardy mentioned towards the close of the last chapter indicate the emphasis that critics have laid upon the artistic qualities of the Wessex novels, their structural excellence. To deal adequately with Hardy's technique would require space beyond the limits of this brief survey. But the subject cannot be entirely disregarded. In the too-little-known essay on " The Profitable Reading of Fiction," which, if reprinted with authorization, would take its place with Henry James's prefaces and the preface to *The Nigger of the Narcissus* among the most important pronouncements by an English novelist upon his art, Hardy noticed the general lack of appreciation of matters of craftsmanship in a novel as compared with the attention devoted to matters of content. It behoves us, therefore, to pay what attention there is room for to this side of his achievement.

At the outset it needs to be observed that it is a mistake to regard Hardy as an innovator. The structure of his novels shows a clarification, generally a simplification, of the Victorian technique; the lavish shapelessness of Thackeray and Dickens is cut down and moulded into symmetry and order; the novel is no longer an *omnium gatherum* of all sorts of episode, incident, and observation. The much-needed reform which he accomplished in this respect obscured from his first generation of admirers the fact that his technique is still in essentials Victorian. Hardy is the last of an old line rather than the forerunner of a new. In his books one finds no such experiments as those of Henry James: the telling of a tale from within the consciousness of a single character (as in *The Ambassadors*) or in strictly scenic form (as in *The Awkward Age*). Hardy's stories never filter to the reader through the mind of an observer and recorder, in the manner of Conrad. He chooses to disregard the multitudinous contrasting facets of life presented to the novelist by actuality. It is an awareness of this that makes almost any tale of Conrad a thing of a thousand profiles and gives its sculpturesque quality to *Nostromo*. That these effects are not employed by Hardy is not to be counted against him. The absence of them goes to show, what we knew already, that he learnt his technique at an earlier period than that of James and Conrad. He is an artist, often a great artist and always an ingenious craftsman — but his art and craft are Victorian.

There have been those who have raised scruples against the justice of the adjective " artistic " as applied to the Wessex novels, and it may be well to deal with these strictures at once. In general such protests have been directed against those books in which the scene lies in great part beyond the country that Hardy has made particularly his own and which depict a part of society with which he is not especially familiar. Enough has been said in the foregoing survey of the novels to indicate sympathy with those who regret the waste of effort upon the romances, or scenes from romances, that transcend for any length of time the boundaries of Wessex.

On the other hand, strangely enough, frequent objections were offered by contemporary reviewers to the lack of verisimilitude in Hardy's portrayal of the Wessex peasantry. Such critics singled out three points in particular: the rather obvious Shakespearean imitation in the drawing of some of the rustic characters; the incredible amount of wit and wisdom concentrated in small gatherings of yokels; and the hybrid nature of the dialogue, part dialect, part standard English. The first objection (if it be an objection) may be granted. There is Shakespearean imitation in some of the rustic scenes, especially in the earlier books. The scene in the church-vault in *A Pair of Blue Eyes;* the drilling of the raw recruits in *The Trumpet-Major;* the constable's pursuit of the skimmity riders in *The Mayor of Casterbridge;* and the constable and his crew in the short story of "The Three Strangers" are instances in point. But the flavour of literary reminiscence has charmed many readers and is not in itself a thing to be deprecated; to catch the tone and manner of Shakespeare's rustic humour is no mean accomplishment. And the scenes and characters inspire a satisfactory answer to the only important questions in judging works of the imagination: Do they please? Are they genuine? Of the second objection it may be said that the lack of a regular education, even the fact of illiteracy, does not preclude the possibility of possessing mother-wit, and often rather sharpens such wit. In part, too, as in Shakespeare, the humour of the scene grows, not out of the wit, but out of the obtuseness of the speakers. Moreover it depends in large part upon Hardy's ironical comments and interpretations. And in any case art is justified in heightening effects that exist, though in more subdued form, in life. Hardy himself has taken the trouble to answer the criticism directed against the compromise that he has employed in his use of dialect. In a letter on "Dialect in Novels" (*The Athenæum,* November 30, 1878) he wrote:

An author may be said to fairly convey the spirit of intelligent peasant talk if he retains the idiom, compass, and characteristic expressions, although he may not encumber the page with obsolete pronunciations of the purely English words, and with mispronunciations of those derived from Latin and Greek. . . . If a writer attempts to exhibit on paper the precise accents of a rustic speaker, he disturbs the proper balance of a true representation by unduly insisting upon the grotesque element.

This is certainly true. Hardy has successfully accomplished a much more difficult effect than the mere phonological reproduction of dialect, which is a feat not above the abilities of any Sam Slick or Josh Billings. And in adopting this compromise he opened the way to a far wider audience than could have been reached by any literary work, however excellent, in dialect form. How few people — to take an example from Hardy's own country — know the beautiful verse of William Barnes, who committed his fame to the keeping of a form of speech, of dignified ancestry it is true, but local and obsolescent. The verdict of entire success now everywhere meted out to Hardy's rustic scenes is the final comment on these adverse criticisms.

Another objection is more serious. It concerns the excessive use of coincidence throughout the novels. We have already had occasion to note how often such freaks of fortune occur in *A Pair of Blue Eyes*. It is needless to give an exhaustive list of instances from other books; but here are a few striking examples. Upon the chance of Fanny's going to the wrong church the whole train of disasters in *Far from the Madding Crowd* follows. Upon the dicing adventures of Wildeve, Christian Cantle and Venn, and Venn's consequent error about the ownership of the guineas, hangs the tragedy of Clym's irreconciliation with his mother, while the last possibility of saving Eustacia was lost by the chance that Captain Vye failed to hand Clym's letter to her. This motive of the unreceived letter plays an equally important part in *Tess*. In that novel there is a whole series of might-have-been-otherwise events, of points where a slight turn in the scale of chance would have mitigated or thwarted the tragedy. Such extraordinary juxtapositions of events have their parallels in each one of the novels. Moreover Hardy often wrings the last drop of improbability out of such situations. The dicing scene in *The Return of the Native,* for example, might have been worked out to the same conclusion and with the same bearing upon the course of events, without such extraordinary fluctuations of fortune and especially without the last two throws (an ace, followed by a blank or zero caused by the die splitting and falling with both cleft surfaces upwards.) An instance of how this sort of scene may be conducted without such absurd exaggeration is the adventure of Rastignac in the gambling-house. Frankly, it must be admitted that Hardy often follows his natural bent towards the mysterious and improbable to the point where he overreaches himself in the employment of coincidence. But two pleas may be entered in his behalf. One — it is hardly valid — is that he never completely shook off the literary influences of his apprenticeship to the school of " sensation novelists " who made abundant use of the same device. The other and stronger plea is the fact that Hardy senses, and in the endeavor to bring it home to the reader exaggerates, the factor of chance in life. His indictment against life is that it is so ordered that such chances as occur again and again in the novels dictate often the misery or happiness of human creatures.

Of the same literary origin as his use of coincidence is Hardy's employment of sensational devices and situations. Of this, too, he never wholly rid himself. *Desperate Remedies*, as we have seen, is filled with such: mystery with regard to birth, burning buildings, murder and a walled-up corpse, midnight spies, mysterious sounds thrice foretelling important events, and much else. In one place the use of capital letters to convey to the reader the excitement of the speaker betrays clearly the influence of Charles Reade. The later books are never so dependent on sensationalism, but most of them offer the same commodity at one time or another in concentrated form: the cliff episode in *A Pair of Blue Eyes;* the rick-burning, Troy's sword-exercise, and the murder of Troy in *Far from the Madding Crowd;* the gambling episode in *The Return of the Native;* the burning of the castle in *A Laodicean;* Clare's sleep-walking with Tess in his arms; and the death of the children in *Jude* are examples that come quickly to mind. Such scenes are admissible in novels of another sort, but in general they are out of accord with the austere control exhibited by Hardy in other respects. Moreover they are in actuality of too rare occurrence to be representative of life; and the novel should reflect the great norm of existence, not the isolated exceptional phenomena. In recording these points of disapproval one must not forget that in the essay referred to at the beginning of this chapter Hardy pleads for a slavish belief in the author on the part of his reader " however profusely he may pour out his coincidences, his marvellous juxtapositions." When all is said, the scattered melodramatic episodes sink to insignificance among the crowd of interesting, picturesque and thrilling scenes that yet remain within the limits of artistic verisimilitude.

ллллллллллг

HENRY JAMES, explaining the reappearance of Christina Light in *The Princess Casamassima,* speaks of " the obscure law under which certain of a novelist's characters, more or less honourably buried, revive for him by a force or whim of their own and ' walk' round his house of art like haunting ghosts." Undoubtedly Hardy was not exempt from this experience. In projecting a series of novels the action of which occurs for the most part within a narrow stretch of country, a district over much of which it is possible to walk in the course of a week-end excursion, there must have been a special temptation to connect the several books together by introducing the same characters into two or more of them. Zola employed this method through a long series of stories dealing with the fortunes of various members of the same family. In the *Comédie Humaine* a vast crowd of people come and go, and there is presented now one phase and now another in the career of various principal personages, with a resultant confusion that requires a sort of guidebook if we are properly to follow the lives of such outstanding characters as, say, Rastignac, Lucien de Rubempré, Vautrin, or the Baron Nucingen. The Barchester novels are similarly, though less complexly, woven together. Thackeray uses such links hardly ever; Dickens, so far as one remembers, only in *Master Humphrey's Clock.* Hardy, except for one purpose, has avoided this pessible mode of procedure, the unity of background being depended on to link the series of tales together. The exceptions occur when some one is introduced as a minor character, to reinforce the impression of time and place, as part of the locality (as it were), in one story who in another story is of psychological importance. Thus Conjurer Trendle, who is a principal actor in " The Withered Arm," is just mentioned in *Tess,* the time and general locality of the two tales being thus fixed as about the same. In *Tess,* too, occurs an amusing anecdote (to be referred to again in the next chapter) of William Dewy's youth, thus connecting that novel with *Under the Greenwood Tree* in which Dewy appears as an old man. Farmer Shinar, one of Fancy Day's lovers in the latter story, appears as one of the agriculturists in *The Mayor of Casterbridge.* Darton, the chief character in " Interlopers at the Knap," is likewise mentioned in that book. And the appearance of Farmer Everdene and " a silent, reserved young man named Boldwood " among Henchard's creditors fixes the date of *The Mayor of Casterbridge* as some fifteen or twenty years earlier than that of *Far from the Madding Crowd*. It is pleasing (glancing ahead for a moment to the poems) to come across a Wessex volunteer in *The Dynasts* named Cantle, for it is a reminder of how old Granfer Cantle in *The Return of the Native* used to recall memories of his warlike youth in "the Bang-up Locals." Again in *The Dynasts* Bob Loveday is mentioned as among the sailors who walked in Nelson's funeral procession; and this brings to mind memories of *The Trumpet-Major*. And the appearance of Solomon Longways connects the epic-drama with the lowly tragedy of *The Mayor of Casterbridge*. Between the short poems and the novels there are several such links. " Tess's Lament " is an attempt (more successful perhaps than some critics have allowed it to be) to render in quintessential form Tess's feelings after Clare's abandonment of her. "The Pine-Planters " is an exquisite reverie upon two motives in *The Woodlanders*. "The Moth-Signal " calls to mind a scene in *The Return of the Native*. "Friends Beyond" and "The Dead Choir " memorialize Tranter Dewy and his fellows in *Under the Greenwood Tree*. The verses called " The Well-Beloved " are a meditation upon the theme illustrated at large in the novel of the same name. There are other less definite connections between the two portions of Hardy's work. He has thus with faint, fine, infrequent touches linked together the persons of his imagination, without ever approaching the point where such links become confusing entanglements.

ⅬⅬⅬⅬⅬⅬⅬⅬ

In the essay already referred to several times, Hardy remarks: "To a masterpiece in story there appertains a beauty of shape, no less than to a masterpiece in pictorial or plastic art"; and he instances *The Bride of Lammermoor* as an almost perfect specimen of form, dwelling also upon the constructive art of Richardson, while questioning the validity of the claim of *Tom Jones* to pre-eminence in this regard. The remark opens up a wide field for discussion concerning the Wessex novels. Only a few outstanding matters can be touched on here.

A certain method of opening his stories — used occasionally by Scott, who, however, did not realize its possibilities — may be observed in Hardy's novels to an extent which makes it almost a mannerism. It is justified, however, by the effect that it produces. The story begins on a road or path along which some person is moving. Here are some typical examples. In *Under the Greenwood Tree* the choir-men are walking along the road; in *Far from the Madding Crowd* Oak meets Bathsheba as she drives along; the first human beings who appear in *The Return of the Native* are Venn and the occupants of his van; *The Mayor of Casterbridge* first presents us with Henchard and his family on their way to the fair-grounds;

in *The Woodlanders* we first see the barber on
his way to the cottage of Marty South; in *Two on
a Tower* it is Lady Constantine in her landau; in *Tess,*
the antiquarian clergyman accosts Durbeyfield on the
road; in "Fellow-Townsmen" Barnet meets Downe
on the turnpike; Farmer Darton is discovered at the
beginning of "Interlopers at the Knap" riding
towards the home of his bride-to-be; Pierston in *The
Well-Beloved* is walking along the Street of Wells as
the story opens; in the second chapter of *A Pair of
Blue Eyes* Smith is seen driving towards the vicarage;
in the second section of "The Withered Arm"
Lodge is discovered driving home with his wife.
These instances are sufficient for our purpose. What is
the effect produced by such a beginning? In almost
every case the reader seems, if it may be so expressed,
to be moving with the protagonists or with those
connected in fortune with them, into the theatre of
action. The scene whereon the coming tragedy or
tragi-comedy is to be displayed is thus gradually un-
folded, the outer country is left behind, the unity of
action is strengthened, and the unity of place. A
similar device is employed in several books in which
there is a sort of prologue in one locality after which
the action moves to another place around which it
clings and which it seldom, sometimes never, leaves
again. Examples of this are: *Desperate Remedies, Far
from the Madding Crowd,* and *The Mayor of Casterbridge.* In *The Woodlanders* the unity of place is almost inviolate; note how the London episode of the

divorce proceedings is reported by letter and how Mrs. Charmond's death on the Continent is narrated by one of the characters. In *The Return of the Native* this unity is absolute and the unfolding of the action uninterruptedly on the heath adds greatly to the impressiveness of a tragedy in which environment plays so overwhelming a part. One should remark also in the same book the swiftness of the blows of Circumstance, for the entire action takes place in a year and a day, thus preserving in some sort the unity of time. The observance of such once-styled " rules " is of course by no means an essential part of the novelist's art, but beyond question in these particular cases it aids greatly in producing the desired effect. Admirable also are such contrivances of structure as that of *The Woodlanders* which begins and closes upon the solitary figure of Marty South, self-sacrificing in the first scene for her father and loyal in the last to the memory of Winterborne. Henchard leaves Casterbridge in the same forlorn and outcast state as that in which he had arrived twenty years before. *The Return of the Native* exhibits at the opening the form of Eustacia upon Rainbarrow and ends with Clym upon the same gaunt hillside. It is undeniable that there is some loss of artistic excellence in *Tess* and particularly in *Jude* in which the action seems to jerk as it moves from place to place.

Just as Hardy gradually leads his reader into the story by means of an opening scene upon the road or by a kind of prologue in one place before the removal of the action to its permanent seat, so does he gradually unfold the appearance and characteristic traits of his principal personages. There are no long, prolegomenous, set descriptions such as occur so often in some other novelists, notably in Balzac. One finds no such full-length character-portraits at the beginning of his books as that of " The Chief " in Meredith's *Vittoria*. Even the sketch of Oak with which *Far from the Madding Crowd* begins is expanded in an exceptional manner. One may contrast the technique of Smollett, Scott, and especially Dickens. Their elaborate descriptions of characters on their first appearance go back through the eighteenth-century essay to the " character-writers " of the seventeenth century. To introduce such full-length portraits into a novel is psychologically bad. One does not really follow this order in observing people. In reality the eye first lights upon some one particular thing — an individuality or oddity of dress or manner or speech — and it is around this quality that other characteristics gradually accumulate. Hardy is well aware of this. He avoids most successfully the common error of describing at once and in great detail the appearance of persons in whom the reader is not yet interested. This is generally accomplished by letting the reader come across the character, as it were, much as any stranger in the book might chance upon him. Very often the scene is at night, or else in some place where shadows veil details. Thus — to take two instances only out of many — Oak passes Bathsheba on the road and the reader is furnished with just so much description of her as could come within Oak's observation of her on that occasion. Again: Eustacia first appears outlined against the sky on Rainbarrow, a slim, romantic figure only. Presently the light of the November bonfire reveals her features fitfully and mysteriously. Her appearance becomes more fully descried by the light in her grandfather's house on her return home. But it is only the next day, by which time our interest is fully aroused, that the morning light enables one to discern clearly her form and features and to read thereon the characteristics of her nature.

In no way are Hardy's sense of proportion and his feeling for relative values more finely shown than in the comparative amounts of detail that are worked into his character-drawing. In all the great novels the full light is thrown upon a few central figures, and even within that narrow circle there are different degrees of illumination. Hardy is here at the opposite pole from Balzac, who portrays not only minor figures but often merely incidental persons, people who are but parts of the background and have no influence upon the course of events — the woman who sells nuts to César Birotteau, for example — with an elaborate care equal often to that expended upon his principal personages. It is amusing to imagine to what lengths of digression the peculiar genius of Balzac or of Dickens would have been led in the portrayal of Eustacia's grandfather, the old sea-faring man, whom Hardy is content to leave quite in the background. Throughout the Wessex novels it would be easy to chart the degrees in the descending scale from such commanding figures as, say, Henchard or Jude or Tess, through secondary people like Farfrae or Phillotson or Boldwood, to the crowd of farmers and merchants and other people of a superior social order, and, apart from them, to the background of rustics. Moreover, in drawing his portraits Hardy practises a rigid exclusion of non-essentials. We hear nothing of Clym's life in Paris and only so much of Smith's journey to the East as is needed in order to understand his relations with Knight and Elfrida. Boldwood's young manhood does not concern the fortunes of Bathsheba and therefore nothing is told of it. A second Mrs. C. C. Clarke might write a " Girlhood of Hardy's Heroines " with opportunities for the display of sentimental fancy equal to those afforded by Shakespeare. What wilful, naughty, high-strung children they must have been! Yet Hardy tells us nothing of their early life. His unbroken rule is to tell just so much of the life-story of his characters as it is necessary to know to follow his theme. Thus, after Tess's departure from Alec, the course of her seducer's life is ignored save for the meeting with the elder Mr. Clare, which is told by Angel to Tess and which, as it brings about Alec's " conversion," is of tremendous importance to her. There was tragedy in the life of Phillotson during the years between the time that he took leave of Jude to study for the ministry and his reappearance as a poor school-master — but of this we hear nothing; it does not concern Jude Fawley. Again: the motives that led Farfrae to come to Casterbridge and the course of his career after Henchard's death are both interesting subjects; but they have no bearing upon Henchard and are consequently omitted. Certainly the historian of *César Birotteau* and *La Maison Nucingen* would not have resisted the temptation to recount the steps by which Henchard made his fortune; but Hardy's reserve is equal to this test also.

There is a similar subordination (though this is more difficult to illustrate) of details to the total effect in the matter of incidents and episodes, and all events are stressed in proportion to their importance for the general theme. To this rule there are two justifiable exceptions. As a means of sustaining interest some spectacular events, such as Knight's accident or the rain-storm on the night of Fanny's burial, are more minutely portrayed than is strictly necessary for the conduct of the story. And there are, of course, the rustic scenes in which the peasants comment upon the doings of their superiors, which are introduced as a sort of interlude.

In many of the novels great care is taken to harmonize the setting with the event that takes place therein. Contrast, for example, Bathsheba's meeting for the first time with each of her three lovers. Oak she first sees while he is occupied with his ewes in the lambing season. Boldwood rides up to her door and

away again impetuously. Troy she encounters on a
dark path and her skirt is caught by his sword. In
The Woodlanders Marty is seen for the first time in
the lonely cottage and for the last time by the lonely
grave. In *A Group of Noble Dames* as night comes
on the stories told by the members of the antiquarian
club become darker in tone. In *Tess* the adjustment
of place and season is accomplished with the highest
art. It is spring-time at the beginning of the tale. Tess
goes to the home of the pseudo-D'Urbervilles in high
summer and returns from Alec amid autumnal decay.
It is summer again on the dairy-farm and winter on
the wedding-day and again at Flintcomb-Ash. So also
the action moves in appropriate places. The initial
tragedy of Tess's life takes place in the gloomy woodland called the Chase; the courtship of Angel and Tess
goes on amid the unconventional, bright sensuousness
of Talbothay's dairy; the wedding-night passes in the
dark ancestral manor-house of the D'Urbervilles and
in the ruined abbey near by; Tess, the deserted wife,
supports herself on the harsh and unsympathetic
Flintcomb-Ash farm; the murder of Alec occurs in a
tawdry seaside boarding-house; and the last night
with Clare passes at Stonehenge, Tess the destined
victim of social conventions sheltering herself in the
ruins of the pagan temple where, thousands of years
before, her ancestors had been sacrificed upon the
altar of a barbarous religion.

The rural setting of the novels in a sequestered
vale of life, though it greatly restricts Hardy's range

of subject and character, possesses corresponding advantages. It confirms the unity of effect. It accounts plausibly for the close interconnections of the various personages. It explains the absence of various conventions that have been imposed on more " advanced " communities and gives ample room for the expression of individuality without the check that arises from the power of the reason when strengthened by convention. Hence it is the appropriate ground for men and women yielding to the dictates of instinct; warm, elemental, vigorous human beings who are close to earth. From the setting, too, comes the sense of detachment and separation from the outside world that makes each novel seem complete in itself and unlike the imaginary scene of many other writers whose novels seem mere fragments of a larger world. There is a consequent loss of breadth, perhaps, but there is a gain in intensity. Analogies suggest themselves from the graphic and plastic arts where certain compositions contain lines that seem to reach out beyond the limits of the subject while certain others are so arranged as to possess only curves that turn harmoniously inward. Hardy, as we have seen, never relies upon the supernatural, yet the remoteness and self-sufficiency of his setting remove him far from the realists. His art sheds a sombre " light that never was on sea or land " over his scene; he is constantly upon the borders of the Unknowable.

If his books are read with proper attention to their technique, it will be admitted, then, that in his

greater works he has realized his own ideal of imparting to masterpieces of story a beauty of shape such
as is found in masterpieces of pictorial or plastic art.
There is a like attention paid to grouping, selection,
subordination, emphasis, and harmonious composition. The lines of the stories may be traced and they
will fall into large, simple, unabrupt curves. The
growth of the story proceeds gradually; the interest
rises towards the centre; and there is an equally
gradual subsidence of emotional tensity at the close.
In these large matters of structure and design Hardy's
art at its best is almost impeccable. But what about
the medium in which he works?

ᴜᴜᴜᴜᴜᴜᴜᴜᴜ

HARDY must not be judged as a " stylist " in the sense
of the word as it is used of De Quincey or Ruskin
or Pater or Meredith or James. His prose narratives do not display that sheer delight in the use of
language for its own sake, beautifully or forcefully
or subtly or cleverly, which is the mark of the vir-
tuoso. He is interested in what he has to say far more
than in the way in which he says it. He is willing at
times to sacrifice elegance and grace to precision. The
aphorisms scattered through the novels (such as the
many comments upon women to be found in *Far
from the Madding Crowd*) are not, like Meredith's
polished jewels, exotics valued for themselves, but are
of importance as integral parts of the writer's theme.
His literary allusions and those to the fine arts are

not learned appendages but are introduced to render more vivid the situation or to cast additional light upon the character he is drawing. If Meredith is an artist in metaphor, then is Hardy equally an artist in simile. The contrast is more real than are most of the comparisons that have been made between the two men. The use of simile is to be expected from so keen an observer as Hardy. A telling number of forced and harsh and ugly similes can easily be gathered from the novels; but they are more than offset by the host of those that are apt and often exquisite. The point to be made here is that just as metaphor in the hands of Carlyle becomes itself a metaphor of his transcendentalism, so is simile appropriate to Hardy, for by his use of this figure of speech he suggests on every page of his writings the intimate interrelation of human beings and human affairs with the natural world around them. Take a single instance of this:

To see her hair was to fancy that a whole winter did not contain darkness enough to form its shadow; it closed over her forehead like nightfall extinguishing the western glow.

There is a cosmic quality in this. With the reference to the fading twilight and to wintry darkness a curtain seems, as it were, to rise for an instant behind Eustacia and we catch a glimpse of the vast, unknown stretch of the universe beyond her. In a moment it falls and we are face to face with humanity again. In the same novel the comparison of Eustacia's sun-lit mouth to a red tulip calls up far-reaching suggestions of a different order, and the tenderness with which the boy holds her hand — " like that of a child holding a captured sparrow " — of a different kind still. It is easy to pass over single instances of these kinds without stopping to analyze them; but as they occur again and again there comes to be a growing impression of how each individual life contains in little the characteristics of the Whole, of how in any small series of events there are implications as wide as the universe. This impression, as we shall see, is one of the most powerful produced by Hardy's poems.

It has just been said that Hardy's is the style, or the absence of style, that comes from a man intent upon what he has to say. From this fact flow two consequences. When he is bored by his subject he becomes, not slip-shod, not hurried and scamping, but plodding, conscientious, sometimes dull. He is then rigid and didactic and it is then that there come those over-technical descriptions to which reference has already been made. Then, too, are found the passages of uninspired philosophizing that remind one of George Eliot. On the other hand, he invariably rises to the heights demanded of great situations in narrative. Knight's accident on the cliff; Fanny's burial; Mrs. Yeobright's return across the heath; Henchard's wedding-gift to his daughter; the Midsummer Eve in the forest; Tess in the Chase; the death of Jude — the insight and strength and exactitude of such scenes are tremendous. Here, as in the large design of the books, so in the choice of words, there is a strict exclusion of non-essentials, a selection of the precise words required. And he has mastered the opposing principles of the exactitude demanded of the naturalist and the power of suggestion expected of the romancer. His descriptive and narrative powers reach their height in the extraordinary prose stage-directions in *The Dynasts*. But he is by no means so nearly faultless in dialogue. This weakness accounts in part for the impression of immaturity made by *A Pair of Blue Eyes* in which much of the story is conveyed in dialogue (a bit of technique that Hardy fell heir to, however unconsciously, from Reade and Collins). The situation between Clym and Eustacia following the boy's revelation of the circumstances of Mrs. Yeobright's death is convincing beyond the abilities of almost any English novelist; the train of circumstances leads unbrokenly and unhesitatingly to the catastrophe; it was in a literal sense a *scène à faire;* but the words put into the mouth of Clym and of his wife lack an undefinable something of reality. They are literary. The vision is not absolute. They are what a husband and wife would be expected to say in such a situation rather than what Clym and Eustacia must necessarily have said on that particular morning. The same is true of the great scene between Clare and Tess on their wedding-night and it might be paralleled in many other places in the novels. Yet even Thackeray, who is a far finer master of dialogue than is Hardy, did not quite succeed in the dialogue of the scene between Rawdon and Becky and Lord

Style

Steyne; and where Thackeray has fallen short of complete success it is no dishonour to Hardy to have nearly failed. Balzac might have succeeded; but who else?

These strictures with regard to dialogue do not hold good of the rustic scenes. There Hardy is uniformly successful. It is almost a paradox to say that in the dialogue that owes most to literary reminiscence he is nearest to life, to the impression of actuality; but it is true of the talk of his yokels. The ease and lightness, the perfect harmonizing of effort with the result achieved, is one proof of how well Hardy knows the country of his birth.

4
The Natural History of Wessex

HARDY knows the Southern counties as Gilbert White knew Selborne; the towns and villages, their history and inhabitants and customs as Mr. Bennett knows the Five Towns. The minutest objects and occurrences of the country-side are as familiar to him as to Richard Jefferies, and his range is far more extensive. He is the natural historian of Wessex. As such he is in lineal descent from Fielding, many of whose scenes and characters belong to Dorset and Somerset. He follows the Brontës, George Eliot, Trollope, William Black, and Blackmore in the development of the literary genre known as "Regionalism" and is thus related to such English writers as Mr. Bennett and Mr. Phillpotts, to the various exploiters of Ireland, the Highlands, Wales, Shropshire, the East Coast, and the Isle of Man; and in France to Henry Bordeaux among others. He knows Wessex as Balzac knew Paris and Touraine, as Scott knew the Border Country, as Dickens knew London. But he never needs to go forth into new localities seeking what has come to be called "local colour," as Dickens went forth, note-book in hand, into Yorkshire. One cannot imagine Hardy subjecting himself to a severe course of "documentation" as did Flaubert. Nor could he have disguised himself, like Zola, as a workman in order to gain experiences of the slums of a great city; or — again like Zola — conscientiously take déjeuner with an actress in order to become acquainted with the demi-monde. But Hardy's knowledge of the life of Casterbridge or Mellstock or Budmouth is kept subservient to the purposes of his story. He reproduces only such portions of a village's multifarious activities as are needed for his theme. There is no such impression of the confusion and bustle of the little world of a small town as we find in Balzac. Gissing knew the East End of London as intimately as Hardy knows Wessex, but there is tragedy in that intimacy, for the slums were forced upon Gissing and, hating the people, he portrayed their life only because it was the material for fiction that he had ready to hand. Hardy, on the contrary, is steeped in, and loves, the heaths and farms and woodlands, the customs and traditions and superstitions among which he lives and which are enshrined in his writings. He describes them, not as the carefully observant tourist would do, from the point of view of an outsider, but as one familiar with them through a lifetime. His knowledge is accurate in detail; but that is not all. He has imaginative sympathy and a consciousness of the close relationship of man and the natural world amidst which he moves and of which he is a part.

Thomas Hardy

Though his mind has been impregnated with modern ideas, his temperament is essentially rustic, primitive, pagan. His description of Angel Clare applies to himself: "Early association with country solitudes had bred in him an unconquerable and almost unreasonable aversion to modern town life." There is no urban element in his nature and therefore a vast field of human experience is almost hidden from him. For Hardy's counsel Meredith might have written the sonnet called "Earth's Secret":

Not solitarily in fields we find
Earth's secret open, though one page is there;
Her plainest, such as children spell, and share
With bird and beast; raised letters for the blind.
Nor where the troubled passions toss the mind,
In turbid cities, can the key be bare.
It hangs for those who hither thither fare,
Close interthreading nature with our kind.

It is quite true, as Hardy writes in his General Preface, that the objection that novels that evolve their action on a circumscribed scene cannot be inclusive in their exhibition of human nature, does not hold good in respect of the elementary passions. But the passions and motives and manners of sophisticated society form no part of his world.

Every book and essay on Hardy devotes much attention to his "treatment of Nature." Three stages in this attitude may be roughly indicated: at first Nature is regarded, with something of the "pathetic fallacy," as a conspirator against Man; later as a fellow-sufferer with Man; and at length Nature gradually disappears from the field of Hardy's interest — in *Jude* entirely so, though there is a recurrence to her in many of the poems.

Passages illustrative of Hardy's powers of observation and description have been quoted by all writers upon him. But no matter how often it has been done no survey of Hardy's achievement can pretend to completeness that does not call attention again to this side of his work. Bearing in mind, however, the great amount that has been written on this subject, one may avoid the temptation to gather together a whole anthology of exquisite word-pictures of heath and orchard and meadowland; of moth and rabbit and hedge-hog and all the creatures of the country; and one may be content with noting a few typical instances only. The mere turning of his pages will quickly supply a hundred more.

Of the dwellers in the woodland he says that they possess " an almost exhaustive biographical or historical acquaintance with every object, animate and inanimate, within the observer's horizon." The remark applies to himself, and his horizon is all Wessex. Throughout the novels the sights and sounds and smells, the birds and beasts, the trees and brooks and flowers, are recorded with a light, deft touch, neither over-scientific and technical, nor inaccurate and vague. No natural phenomenon is too grand for his pen. He watches the motions of the constellations and tells the hour by the position they have attained. He records the progress of the storm, the contrasting and increasing brilliance of the lightning, the various rollings of the thunder. Nor is any event too small for his sympathy. The humble toad seeking shelter and the spiders that drop from the ceiling are signs of the coming storm. He notes the " musical breathings " of the pine which begin as soon as the young tree is set in the ground. He describes the " tiny crackling of the dead leaves " as they return to their proper position after the passage of feet over them. As a sign of coming spring he records that " birds began not to mind getting wet." What intimate affection is in that remark! Humorous but loving comprehension of a dog's nature is seen in the account of the well-meant but disastrous exertions of Oak's younger sheep-dog. He is tolerant of the only half-angry bull that annoys Elizabeth-Jane and admires the splendour of its puzzled rage when it is trapped in the barn. The ways of cows are revealed in *Tess* and of sheep in *Far from the Madding Crowd*. With a humour that is akin to pathos yet has in it nothing of Sterne's sentimentality he narrates the death of the Durbeyfields' horse. Cats are not so highly honoured as they deserve to be in the Wessex novels; but it is pleasant to know that Max Gate has sheltered several and that they have been as much loved by Hardy as by Samuel Butler and George Moore.

He never tires of recording the changes in the animal and vegetable worlds as the seasons pass over them. He sets down in detail " the change from the handsome to the curious which the features of a wood undergo at the ingress of the winter months." The urge and stir of returning life in the spring never fail to move him. He contrasts the sound of rain-drops as they fall on different kinds of ground: " Sometimes a soaking hiss proclaimed that they were passing by a pasture, then a patter would show that the rain fell upon some large-leafed root crop, then a paddling plash announced the naked arable." He can differentiate between the various sounds of the wind as it blows through trees of different species, and as it passes over various parts of the heath. Signs of coming rain and of returning fair weather are clear to him. From him we can learn the contrasting appearance of bonfires according to the sort of wood or brush that is being burnt in them. He loves fires — particularly at night. Night in all her moods is familiar to him; and dawn no less than twilight. One of the most beautiful passages in the novels is the description of dawn on the Froom meadows when Angel Clare is reminded of the Resurrection hour. Another almost equally lovely is the picture of the woods at the hour of Bathsheba's awakening there. And as a picture of the decline of day turn to the description of the forest at nightfall in *The Woodlanders*. In the beautiful recent poem " Afterwards " Hardy voiced his hope that if, when he is gone, men remember him at all, it will be as one who noticed the loveliness of the spring, to whom the hawk and the thorn were familiar sights, who strove to protect the little creatures of the country-side from harm, and who had an eye for the mysteries of the full-starred heavens.

ᴜᴜᴜᴜᴜᴜᴜᴜᴜᴜᴜ

HARDY is wont, in a manner more recently associated with his disciple Eden Phillpotts, to centre his stories around some one or other of the trades and occupations of Wessex. In *Tess* we watch the life of the Great Dairies: the milking, skimming, churning, cheese-making, and the minor occupations of the dairy-hands such as the charmingly described task of uprooting the few strands of garlic that were tainting the milk. Later in the same book one reads of harsher and less picturesque work like "hacking," reed-drawing, and threshing. *Far from the Madding Crowd* is set amidst the cares and pleasures of shepherds: lambing, washing and shearing, the shearing-supper (an unforgettable scene), and the sheep-fair. Bathsheba appears at the corn-market, an episode that connects this book with *The Mayor of Casterbridge* in which the corn-and-hay trade is depicted. Life in the timber and orchard districts is the background of *The Woodlanders;* quarriers and stone-sawyers appear in *The Well-Beloved;* furze-cutting is the austere and lonely occupation of many of the peasants in *The Return of the Native.* The story of *The Trumpet-Major* moves in and around an old flouring-mill. The questionable trade of smuggling is amusingly portrayed in "The Distracted Preacher." The

doings of the old string band (not a trade but formerly an important occupation) forms a large part of
the theme of *Under the Greenwood Tree*.

ⅬⅬⅬⅬⅬⅬⅬⅬⅬⅬⅬ

CUSTOMS change slowly in Wessex. In "The Fid-
dler of the Reels " Hardy says that 1851, the year of
the Great Exhibition, " formed . . . an extraordinary chronological frontier" between old ways
and new. Many of the Southern folk, journeying up
to London, then saw the outer world for the first
time. From that period on, old habits began to disappear and new ways, the ways of the drab, undifferentiated, board-school English labourer everywhere, began to creep in. The dialectical peculiarities
began to be levelled out and many of them are now
becoming obsolete. The older people who use them
are snubbed by the younger generation educated at
the National Schools. Hardy has commented upon
these changes in the preface to his volume of selections
from the poems of William Barnes. But modern ways
are not yet completely dominant, for many traditional
customs still linger, " only in a metamorphosed or
disguised form." In *Who's Who* Hardy set down
" old church and dance music " among his hobbies or
recreations, for he took an affectionate interest in
these memorials of the old times. The lovely old custom of the Christmas " wakes " is described in detail
in *Under the Greenwood Tree* and is the theme of
the touching poem " The Dead Choir." Allusions to

hymn-books and to the instruments of the players occur constantly. The vicar's training of one such choir forms an amusing scene in *Two on a Tower*. Hardy speaks often of old hymn-tunes and psalm-tunes, notably in the inn scene in *The Mayor of Casterbridge* when Henchard forces the singers to perform the terrible commination psalm. No English writer has described the joy of dancing with more gusto than Hardy. He speaks of the twisting of old folk-airs and the doctoring of them so that they reappear as new music-hall ditties, and of "country jigs, reels, and 'Favorite Quick Steps' of the last century — some mutilated remains of which even now reappear as nameless phantoms in new quadrilles and gallops, where they are recognized by the curious."

Instances of such decayed survivals of old folk-customs are common in the novels. The club-revel or "club-walking" on the Tuesday after Whitsunday which forms the opening scene of *Tess* is mentioned several times elsewhere by Hardy. It is a folk-survival, the "club" being a degenerate form of the old May Day dance. "Fragments of Teutonic rites to divinities whose names have been forgotten," he says in *The Return of the Native,* "seem . . . to have survived mediaeval doctrine." Two chapters in the novel just named form a *locus classicus* for students of folk-drama. These contain an account of the Christmas Mummers'-Play of Saint George as it was still acted annually about 1840. Typical of the last stages of folk-custom is the way in which the party assembled at Mrs. Yeobright's received the performance:

> The remainder of the play ended. . . . Nobody commented, any more than they would have commented upon the fact of mushrooms coming in autumn or snowdrops in spring. They took the piece as phlegmatically as did the actors themselves. It was a phase of cheerfulness which was, as a matter of course, to be passed through every Christmas; and there was no more to be said.

Folk-play is the last stage in the process of degeneration from sacrifice through cult. It has here been reached. Similar survivals that are recorded are the skimmington or skimmity-ridings ("satiric processions with effigies") of which a full account occurs in *The Mayor of Casterbridge* and to which there is an allusion in the poem "The Fire at Tranter Sweatley's." It has been reported that a skimmington took place in a Dorset village in 1884. In another remote district, it may be added, a skimmity-ride was in progress as late as the summer of 1917 when it was broken up by the police. This cruel custom seems to have arisen in the early years of the seventeenth century as one of the methods of dealing with witches. In earlier instances a man and woman impersonated the couple who were caricatured, whereas in Hardy's reproductions of the custom effigies are made that grossly satirize the unfortunate people. A good example of the more primitive form may be found towards the end of Heywood and Brome's *Late Lancashire Witches* (1634), a play that is a mine of superstitions about witchcraft. Returning to Hardy, one may note the pretty custom of the wedding march around the village or hamlet which takes place in two of the novels. The signal at the outbreak of a fire is the ringing of the church bells backwards. When a death occurs it is announced by the tolling of the bell with a system of changes according to the age and sex of the deceased. These two uses of the bells still survive in some districts. A barbarous relic of a less civilized age is the wife-selling episode with which *The Mayor of Casterbridge* begins. It has been objected that such an occurrence is too improbable to form the basis of a novel's plot. But Havelock Ellis has gathered together in the sixth volume of his *Studies in the Psychology of Sex* many examples of this custom and other well-authenticated cases in England in the nineteenth century are recorded elsewhere. A still grimmer relic of the past is the burial of a suicide at the cross-roads with a stake driven through his heart, which is the subject of the short story of " The Grave at the Handpost."

ununununununu

MANY superstitions survived in Wessex in Hardy's earlier years and have even yet not entirely disappeared. " These smouldering village beliefs," says Hardy, are " sentiments which lurk like moles underneath the visible surface of manners." The Wessex novels are a mine for the folk-lorist and Hardy has been cited by many such as a recognized authority on the subject. Tess and her mother represent the contrast between the younger generation whose belief has been undermined by education, though by no means obliterated as yet, and the elder with its " fast-perishing lumber of superstition, folk-lore, dialect, and orally transmitted ballads." " Fast-perishing " quite probably; but still to be found in out-of-the-way districts where there is even to-day implicit trust in charms as remedies for tooth-ache, St. Vitus's dance, and other ills, and where old-fashioned farmers still prefer the services of a " charmer " to those of a veterinary when their cattle are ill. A collection of some of the relics of ancient credulity that are recorded by Hardy sheds light upon a side of his work over which critics have passed without detailed comment.

The best known of these superstitions and the one that from the time of Theocritus has been most often turned to account in imaginative literature is the melting of a wax image, shaped to represent an enemy, the life of the enemy fading away with the melting of the image. The most familiar example of this theme in English literature is of course Rossetti's *Sister Helen.* The reader may like to be reminded of the charm which Nance Redferne mutters over the clay image, stuck full of pins, of James Device in Ainsworth's *Lancashire Witches,* a romance founded upon the same documents that suggested the theme of their play to Thomas Heywood and Richard Brome. Later in that wild romance the witch causes the grave-digger to put in the ground an image of the

woman she hates, saying "Bury it deep, and as it
moulders away, may she it represents pine and
wither." The terrific nature of this bit of folk-belief
appealed to Hardy and he uses it twice. When Henchard is experiencing the rapid decline of his fortunes
he wonders whether some one has been shaping an
image of him and setting it before the fire. The idea
is used terribly and dramatically in *The Return of the
Native* where Susan Nunsuch melts the image of
Eustacia on the very evening of the latter's death. The
same woman, on an earlier occasion, had pricked
Eustacia's arm and drawn her blood as a means to
stop the suspected bewitching of her children. Had
no blood come it would have been proof positive that
Eustacia was a witch. Thus, a character in Ainsworth's book declares that "your witch should be
put to every ordeal. She should be scratched with pins
to draw blood from her," etc. And in the poem
" A Witch " by Hardy's fellow-townsman, William
Barnes, one reads:

> An' I've a-heärd the farmer's wife did try
> To dawk a needle or a pin
> In drough her wold hard wither'd skin,
> An' draw her blood, a-comèn by:
> But she could never vetch a drap,
> For pins would ply an' needles snap
> Ageän her skin; an' that, in coo'se,
> Did meäke the hag bewitch em woo'se.

Witches and devils are the familiar neighbours of the
Wessex yokels. Dr. Fitzpiers in *The Woodlanders* is

charged with having sold his soul to the devil — the
usual accusation brought by the ignorant and the
credulous against one of superior intellectual attain-
ments, especially if he is an empiricist. The exhausted
condition of the mare which in reality Fitzpiers had
used secretly is explained as being due to its having
been "hag-ridden." The older inhabitants of the
woodland tell strange tales of sights seen in times
past, of witches black and white. The beautiful Vale
of Blackmore is said to teem with beliefs in " green-
spangled fairies that ' wickered ' at you as you passed."
The fact that Barnes is comparatively little known
will excuse one for offering part of his charming little
poem " The Veairies " as an illustration of this. Long
years ago the fairies used to come to the house of the
narrator's grandfather where they danced upon the
floor around the fire. One night they found a keg of
mead and one fairy drank so much that he could not
remember the words that had to be said to make him
small enough to pass through the keyhole:

> He got a-dather'd zoo, that after all
> Out t'others went an' left èn back behind.
> An' after he'd a-beät about his head
> Ageän the keyhole till he were half dead,
> He laid down all along upon the vloor
> Till gramfer, comèn down, unlocked the door:
> An' then he zeed èn ('twer enough to frighten èn)
> Bolt out o' door, an' down the road lik' lightenèn.

In other poems Barnes makes equally delightful use
of these beliefs.

Thomas Hardy

Hardy touches the borders of the supernatural in "The Withered Arm" where there is a hint, and a hint only, of a possible rationalistic explanation of the incubus. (The belief that a witch could blast or wither a limb is an old one; the charge was brought by Richard III against Jane Shore.) In the same story Conjuror Trendle recommends to the afflicted heroine that she lay the withered member across the neck of a man newly hanged. The idea here would seem to be that the vitality of the man just dead, passing out through the wounded portion of his body, will have a restorative effect upon the ailing limb. In former times the same cure was often used for skin diseases and for epilepsy. The lonely dwellings of such conjurors are found, or were to be found till recently, in various parts of Wessex.

Bodements and omens are looked for by the peasantry on all occasions. The breaking of a key or a looking-glass is a dreadful sign. A ringing in the left ear or the sight of a magpie foreshadows a coming murder. As Tess is returning from her sojourn at the Chase a thorn-prick upon her chin gives her great concern. After the wedding of Tess and Clare, as they are departing in the afternoon upon their honeymoon, the cock crows thrice, and the alarmed household endeavour to explain away this grim portent by holding that it is a mere forecast of change in the weather. On several occasions Tess hears the rumble of the spectral D'Urberville coach — which foretells coming disaster. The maidens in *Under the Green-*

wood Tree follow the directions in the "witch's book" in order to catch a glimpse of their future husbands; and in *The Woodlanders* there is a scene of wonderful sensuous charm in which the young girls of the neighbourhood go to the forest on Old Midsummer Eve for this purpose. Bathsheba Everdene divines the future by means of a Bible and a key (as in Heywood's *Wise Woman of Hogsden*) and Conjuror Trendle by looking into the cloudy white of an egg. This last method of "scrying" is a substitute for the more usual crystal-gazing. A copy of *The Compleat Fortune-Teller* or some other such book was often in the possession of peasant families; Joan Durbeyfield stood in such awe of this book that she feared to leave it in the house over night and had it put in the wood-shed every evening. There are many superstitions connected with death; in "Interlopers at the Knap," for instance, we see the sister, after the death of her brother (which happens during the night), slip out of the house and passing along the row of bee-hives wake each swarm in turn; were that not done the bees, too, would die. In the brief tale of "An Imaginative Woman" Hardy connects folk-beliefs with the possibility, admitted by modern science, of pre-natal influence upon physical characteristics, and turns the idea to the uses of irony. Similar cases are recorded in great number in the final volume of Havelock Ellis's *Studies in the Psychology of Sex*. And as an instance of the venerableness of the belief among the English peasantry, the following scrap of dialogue in Lyly's *Mother Bombie* (I, i) may be quoted:

> *Memphio:* Rascall, doest thou imagine thy mistress naught of her body?
> *Dromio:* No, but fantasticall of her mind; and it may be, when this boy was begotten she thought of a foole, and so conceiued a foole.

Hardy records many superstitions of a less sombre sort than those noted in the preceding paragraphs. In *Jude* Vilbert, the quack doctor, sells love-philtres distilled from the juice of doves' hearts. (One recalls that " dust of doves' hearts " is listed by Burton in *The Anatomy of Melancholy,* among love-potions.) Vilbert, like Venn the reddleman and the numerous conjurors, is himself a survival from the far past. Christian Cantle, the "slack-twisted, slim-looking maphrotight fool" of *The Return of the Native,* had the misfortune to be born when there was no moon, thus amply confirming the old saying "No moon, no man." (The antiquity of this belief is shown by the remark of a character in Glapthorne's play, *The Lady Mother:* "Have you then ever seen such another monster? He was begott surely in the wane of the moon.") When Farmer Crick's cows (in *Tess*) do not give their milk abundantly various explanations are offered. " 'Tis because there's a new hand come among us," says one. " I've been told that it goes up into their horns at such times," a dairy-maid suggests; but a bright-minded fellow refutes this by pointing out that the cows whose horns are cut off

are as ungenerous as the rest. " Folks," says Farmer
Crick, " we must lift up a stave or two — that's the
only cure for't." Upon which " the band of milkers
. . . burst into melody — in purely business-like
tones, it is true, and with no great spontaneity." Apparently the milk then came in satisfactory quanti-
ties. On another occasion the butter will not " come."
" Perhaps somebody in the house is in love," one hand
remarks; and consultation with various neighbouring
conjurors is suggested. A pleasant interlude in *Tess* is
the tale of William Dewy of Mellstock (the same
person who appears as an old man in *Under the
Greenwood Tree*.) In his youth he charmed a bull by
playing on his fiddle as he ran away from it; but he
could not manage to climb the fence because to do
so he had to stop playing, until he hit upon the plan
of playing the " 'Tivity Hymn," when the bull, hear-
ing the familiar melody and thinking it must be
Christmas-Eve, knelt down, and before it realized
that it had been fooled Dewy was safely over the
fence. The same charming bit of folk-belief is employed for a very different purpose in one of Hardy's
most moving poems, " The Oxen ":

> Christmas Eve, and twelve of the clock.
> " Now they are all on their knees,"
> An elder said as we sat in a flock
> By the embers in hearthside ease.
>
> We pictured the meek mild creatures where
> They dwelt in their strawy pen,

Nor did it occur to one of us there
To doubt they were kneeling then.

So fair a fancy few would weave
In these years! Yet, I feel,
If someone said on Christmas Eve,
" Come; see the oxen kneel,

" In the lonely barton by yonder coomb
Our childhood used to know,"
I should go with him in the gloom,
Hoping it might be so.

A mediaeval legend analogous to this belief forms the subject of the poem called " The Lost Pyx," which gives one traditional explanation of the origin of the strange stone pillar at the head of Blackmore Vale called " Cross-and-Hand," another explanation of which occurs in *Tess*.

Education has not so much rooted out these old beliefs as it has hidden them away beneath a mantle of shamefacedness and pretended scepticism. This fact is well illustrated by the conference that Henchard has with the conjuror and weather-prophet near Casterbridge, whose clients feign to consult him merely as a whim but who is consoled for the superficial irony of their manner towards him by his confidence in their fundamental belief in his supernatural powers.

The foregoing account of the customs and superstitions recorded in the Wessex novels must not be permitted to give a false impression of the place and prominence they occupy therein. Hardy is no mere anthropologist or folk-lorist. These quaint and curious beliefs are never introduced into the stories for their own sakes alone. They are a part of the " atmosphere," of the " local colour " (to use two well-worn terms at once) of the novels and contribute their quota to the total effect much as do the descriptions of the natural features of the country-side.

5

Men and Women: Peasants

T H E peasants who cling to the beliefs which we
have been discussing do not form a class completely
apart from the other characters in the Wessex novels,
for by almost imperceptible gradations, through such
persons as Oak and Winterborne, the background
or chorus of yokels is connected with the principal
characters who are higher in the social scale. Nevertheless there are traits in the peasantry which differentiate that class from the rest.

Though they possess some qualities in common
among themselves the rustics are often individualized. Hardy has protested more than once against the
city-man's view of the undifferentiated " Hodge."
He contributed an illuminating letter on this and
kindred subjects to *Longman's Magazine,* July, 1879
(" The Dorsetshire Labourer ".) In *A Pair of Blue
Eyes* he insists that it is only in cities that the attrition
is so great as to change the unit Self into a fraction of
the larger unit Class. In *Tess* he remarks that these
rustics are " beings of many minds, beings infinite in

difference; some happy, many serene, a few depressed, one here or there bright even to genius, some stupid, others wanton, others austere." The importance of these people varies with the social strata in which the several stories are set. In *Under the Greenwood Tree* we are in the midst of them; in *The Woodlanders* they play a great part; in *The Return of the Native* rather less; in *Far from the Madding Crowd* and still more in *The Mayor of Casterbridge* they serve rather as part of the background and as a sort of chorus that observes and comments upon events; in *Tess*, save in the dairy-farm scenes, the humour associated with them is becoming acrid — there is grimness in the picture of John Durbeyfield; in *Jude* there is hardly a trace of interest in them, and with their disappearance goes also the humour that accompanied them.

The lives of such men and women are close to earth. They live among the sights and sounds and smells of the natural world. Their being is permeated with them. Consider the description of Winterborne which admirers of Hardy have always delighted to quote:

He looked and smelt like Autumn's very brother, his face being sunburnt to wheat-colour, his eyes blue as corn-flowers, his sleeves and leggings dyed with fruit-stains, his hands clammy with the sweet juice of apples, his hat sprinkled with pips, and everywhere about him that atmosphere of cider which at its first return each season has such an indescribable fascination for those who have been born and bred among the orchards.

One could parallel this passage with others showing peasants among their lambs and ewes, or cutting furze upon the heath, or milking, or threshing, or what you please. They are part of the landscape. They are thoroughly at ease in their world. The signal for an assignation is a stone thrown into a pool imitating the sound of a plunging frog. Another is a moth let loose into a room to beat itself against the lamp. Oak tells the hours by the grand wheel of the constellations. He recognizes the signs of coming rain. He is alert and efficient when confronted with Bathsheba's flatulent sheep. There is no self-consciousness in this knowledge. The peasants lead unspeculative lives close to Nature, never rebelling against Circumstance. If they complain at all — and it is only the feeble among them that do so — it is usually of small physical ills of little moment: Thomas Leaf of his lack of brains (of which he is rather proud than otherwise), William Worm of his deafness, Christian Cantle of his cowardice, and so on. Hardy shows no concern for their " social condition." Often he seems to be out of sympathy with the advance of so-called education, believing that the National Schools obliterate more of value than they give. He lays no stress upon their poverty; in fact in the article referred to above he declares that their misery has been much over-estimated. It is the rustics in the Wessex novels who are happy, for the secret of happiness, as is said in *The Woodlanders*, lies in limiting the aspirations. They are quietists without being aware of the fact. Not that they are necessarily unintelligent. Many are shrewd, some witty, nearly all unconsciously humorous. The humour, as we have seen, is merely an exaggeration, touched with literary reminiscence and artistically justifiable, of qualities to be met with in real life. Often of course they are not so much humorous as the cause of humour in Hardy who juxtaposes their primitive manners and quaint conceits to the ideas and behaviour of more educated people. Their humour consists largely in comments upon the broad, general experiences of humanity: birth, and courtship, and marriage, and death, and success or failure in enterprise. To a great degree it depends upon homely perversions of the sort of learning that, heard Sunday after Sunday all their lives, has become part of themselves — the moral and devotional exhortations of their clergymen, the more picturesque portions of the Scriptures and the Prayer-book ("My scripture manner, which is my second nature," says Joseph Poorgrass), and the good old unsophisticated hymns the staves of which they lift with such a good will.

ᘁᘁᘁᘁᘁᘁᘁ

AMONG those who play a prominent part yet are of secondary importance there is one class of men who stand apart from the rest: the clergy. Hardy's portrayal of them, like George Eliot's, has been a subject for frequent adverse comment, especially during the years when the novels were appearing. It is quite incorrect to say that he is uniformly hostile towards them. Towards the Establishment, vested with social, political, and intellectual prestige, and containing traces of former persecuting privilege, he is consistently and defensibly hostile. But his individual clergymen fall into two well-defined groups. On the one hand are the sincere, ardent, hard-working believers who exercise an energetic, practical, humane influence upon their people; on the other hand, the insincere, generally younger, men who enter the church as a means of social and intellectual advance. The elder Mr. Clare is portrayed with a gentle sympathy untouched by the remotest irony; his portrait is worthy of comparison with those of the ministers of the gospel drawn by Chaucer and Dryden and Goldsmith. Mr. Raunham in *Desperate Remedies* not only gives sensible advice to the Grayes but is capable of directing the work of salvage at the fire. Mr. Maybold in *Under the Greenwood Tree* behaves in a very manly fashion towards Fancy Day. Mr. Torkingham in *Two on a Tower* is a sensible person though a little in awe of his bishop; it is this latter characteristic only that is mildly satirized. Hardy denies any satiric intent in his portrayal of the Bishop of Melchester in this novel; but he has not conquered his prejudices and one cannot but feel that the picture is a caricature. But on the whole all these clerics must be set off as counterbalances against such men as the worldly Mr. Swancourt in *A Pair of Blue Eyes* (a prevalent and very human type) ; Mr. Cope in the short story " For

Conscience's Sake "; the two elder brothers of Angel Clare; and especially the two sons of a drunken father in "A Tragedy of Two Ambitions." Hardy does not always remain clear-sighted and fair. There is angry satire in his portrait of the vicar in *Tess*. And in the powerful short story just referred to one of the brothers remarks to the other:

> " To succeed in the Church, people must believe in you, first of all, as a gentleman, secondly as a man of means, thirdly as a scholar, fourthly as a preacher, fifthly, perhaps, as a Christian."

This is not only bad art (for it is the writer who speaks here, perhaps jestingly, through the mouth of a character who cannot even be imagined as uttering such sentiments); it is manifestly unjust. In such general indictments of the motives that now-a-days draw young men into the ministry Hardy recalls and exaggerates the opinions of George Eliot. It is noteworthy, finally, that in several of the most important novels there is practically no mention of religion or of religious usage at all.

Little attention is paid to the other professional classes. The architects who figure so largely in the earlier books have of course their interest as individuals, but the fact of their profession is of autobiographic, not of psychological, interest. Lawyers are hardly ever heard of, save incidentally as in the divorce proceedings in *The Woodlanders*. Fitzpiers is the only physician who plays a prominent part, and he is drawn rather as an intellectualist in general than with particular regard to his profession. As for the crowds of merchants and farmers, their fate depends upon their temperament and circumstances far more than upon their calling.

ᴜɴᴜɴᴜɴᴜɴᴜ

EDUCATION, widening their mental horizon, has entered in greater or less degree into the lives and characters of most of the leading personages of the novels; and with knowledge come sorrow and complexity.

To understand Hardy's conception of women one must relate it to an important part of his general metaphysic, premising that he himself has indicated that this metaphysic is to be regarded as purely tentative. The enormous number of marital complexities in the novels and short stories and poems is due to the connection of the sexual relation with his general thought. It must be remarked what a little part such Balzacian passions as greed or ambition play in Hardy's world. They are superficial and in a measure conventional passions, a product of civilization. And in his world we are equally far from Meredith's or James's subtle analyses of the delicate motives of refined and artificial people. The love-instinct, on the contrary, reaches to the core of human nature; and the problem of that instinct becomes almost an obsession with him. Troubles arising out of both regular connections and illicit unions are constant. There are at least a dozen seductions in the books. To Hardy's credit it must be said that he does not mince matters.

He had to permit certain concessions in the first magazine versions of several of the novels, but in their final form we meet with frankness and no prudery. It is important to consider here his views on marriage. In both his novels and his poetry Hardy's thoughts revolve frequently around the comic or tragic irony of the mischances of the marital relation; he broods more than most men do, though not more than the evidence warrants, upon the penalties attaching to mis-mating. At the root of his polemics are his sense of the injustice of imposing a permanent bond as the penalty for a passing desire and his knowledge of the numberless instances in which love has been stifled by obligation. But two questions suggest themselves: Just what remedy does Hardy propose? And: Does he imagine that a mere " return to Nature " would be a practicable solution in the modern world? On the whole he seems to advocate merely a greater freedom of divorce; and the development of sentiment during the last thirty years has been in line with his ideas. His final opinion is well summarized in a postscript to the preface to *Jude*. A marriage, he says, " should be dissolvable as soon as it becomes a cruelty to either of the parties— being then essentially and morally no marriage." He protests in *Life's Little Ironies* against marriages of convenience, especially between persons of very different ages. " The necessity of getting life-leased at all costs, a cardinal virtue which all good mothers teach," leads to such unhappy and unsympathetic unions as that depicted in " An

Imaginative Woman." In another tale in the same
collection he speaks of the belief of " the British par-
ent that a bad marriage with its aversions is better
than free womanhood with its interests, dignity, and
leisure." Two notes, added in the recent definitive
edition of his writings, are protests against the old
de rigueur ending of a story with a marriage and life
happy ever after. These notes may be found at the
close of " The Distracted Preacher " and at the point
in *The Return of the Native* where Thomasin an-
nounces her engagement to Venn. Marriage, he says
elsewhere, is not the goal of life, but a milestone on
the path. Yet it does not necessarily bring unhappiness. There is tragedy enough in all conscience; but
it comes from mis-mating, not from mating; from
accepting as a lasting feeling what in many cases is
but a momentary impulse. The true solution comes
when good-fellowship is added to love. " The com-
pound feeling," he writes with grave beauty towards
the close of *Far from the Madding Crowd,* " proves
itself the only love which is strong as death." Nowhere do we find either a sentimentalizing of love (as
in Scott), or an intellectualizing (as in Meredith),
or an idealization (as in Browning) ; but a firm acceptance of it for what it is — a physical passion, a
sexual attraction, carrying with it the hope, but only
the hope, of a permanent bond of affection based on
common interests and common ideas. Hardy is here
much more in line with the female novelists of the
nineteenth century than with the male. If in the mar-

riage of Fancy Day and Dick Dewy and of some other couples, notably Grace and Fitzpiers, there are suggestions and more than suggestions of coming unhappiness, no such clouds overcast the marriage of Bathsheba and Oak or that of Farfrae and Elizabeth-Jane which was, Hardy records, uniformly happy. And perhaps it does not bring the matter to too personal a close to note that in the verses called " A Poet " — and the allusion is unmistakable — Hardy asked that the memory of him should be that " two thoughtful women loved him well."

On the whole, however, Hardy's attitude towards women is unfavourable; his opinion of them is bitter. They have many good qualities of heart, but they are fickle and vain, insincere, conscienceless, and seductive. Almost all are passionate, and passion leads invariably to grief. The Brontë sisters and George Eliot had led the way away from the Rowenas and Doras and Amelias of earlier fiction. Meredith, too, had broken the old bonds, but, as contrasted with Hardy, he had over-intellectualized his women. His revolt from sentimentalism and from " the charity of chivalry " was in itself an unconscious yielding to sentiment. In Hardy there is nothing of this.

It has not hitherto been remarked how few children appear in the Wessex novels. It is almost a childless world. Even the many love-children are either grown-up, or play a passive part, or die in infancy. The boy who holds Eustacia's hand as a reward for the services rendered her is a precocious youth unconvincingly drawn. The wretched son of Jude and Arabella suffers, among his many other miseries, from the responsibility, one is tempted to say, of being an allegory. Nowhere is there shown such a healthy, normal relationship as that existing between Richmond Roy and his son Harry. But Meredith had the intimate pleasures of association with his son Arthur before their alienation; and Hardy had no children. Is it fanciful to find in this strange and great omission from Hardy's world one reason for the lack of sweetness in the novels? They are often tender and almost always sympathetic; but they are hardly ever sweet. The absolute omission, of which something has already been said, of all non-essentials necessitated the sacrifice of beautiful opportunities. What was Clym's childhood with his strong-minded and formidable but devoted mother? What was Elizabeth-Jane's life with her kindly sailor-father before she appears at Casterbridge? What, even, were the happy hours that Jude and Sue must have spent with their babies?

The omission is the more remarkable in that the function of child-bearing is the central idea in Hardy's view of women. The business of life is to reproduce life; existence is for the sake of existence. Nature, seeking only to prolong the species, has given this function pre-eminently to woman. Hence woman's instinctive assertion of charm against which the intelligence of man revolts but to which his instincts succumb. What has been called the " capriciousness " of Hardy's women is in reality their immediate and instinctive obedience to emotional impulse, without the corrective control of the intelligence. It is one form through which the All-Mover, the Prime Impulse, works, darkly, unreasoningly. What in these women seems a lack of volition is due to their being possessed by the Will. Love, the sexual attraction, forms the chief motive in Hardy's tragedies both because its passionate force brings out the individual in most uncontrolled revolt against the social norm and because it embodies the conflict of reason and intuition. The earlier novels, in which these ideas were already implicit, were written before Schopenhauer was known in England, but the resemblances between the later books, notably *Jude,* and the teachings of the German philosopher are so close as almost to rule out of consideration the possibility of their being due simply to coincidence. Hardy's women are all of one type, differing only in degree. They are essentially Cyrenaics. The principle of calculation they are unaware of. The happiness of the moment blinds them to the hypothetical disaster of the morrow. They ask for the intensity of experience in the present rather than for the future satisfaction that comes from self-control. Those who consider Hardy "voluptuous" fail to see that (to borrow Swinburne's simile) like a mediaeval preacher, while on the one side he places Love on the other he places Death. It is the difference in degree of this impulsiveness that makes Hardy's women individuals. There are some women of the lower social order, living close to Nature and meeting bravely the struggle of daily life, who in a measure reject the attributes of sex and represent, as it were, an undifferentiated humanity. Thomasin and Marty South are examples of this type. There are shades of difference between women who are in essentials much alike, as between the worldly and disillusioned Mrs. Charmond and the educated but not ignoble Grace, the one out of harmony with her environment, the other reaching back towards an accord which has been marred, though not as yet destroyed, by contact with the outer world. In some there are approximations to judiciousness and self-control. The determination of Bathsheba to manage her possessions independently gives her a measure of such judiciousness. In Eustacia there is a force that seeks to compel circumstances into accord with the world of her dreams. And then there is the gentle bewilderment of Tess. And there is the downright animalism of Arabella. Mr. Duffin has set down in diagrammatic form the relationship of the leading women with their several lovers, and Mr. Hedgcock gives a list of some thirteen women who play fast and loose with thirty-three lovers. The extremes meet in *Jude the Obscure*. Arabella, as we have seen, is the tool of the Will-to-Live. She is thus free from the prudent reserves that retard, though they do not successfully control, the love-instinct in women of more education like Eustacia. Sue, suggestions of whose self-control are seen in Elizabeth-Jane and

Ethelberta, represents the modern growth of self-
regardfulness and intellectuality as opposed to the
older complacent obedience to instinct. But even Sue
breaks down in the end.

Fundamentally the same qualities, characteristic
of undifferentiated human nature, are found in
Hardy's men as in his women, though with a wider
distribution of self-control and with an at least occasional triumph of reason over instinct. Setting aside
the numerous young men whose characters are not
yet fixed, one notes that his men fall roughly into
three classes. On the one side are the sensualists of
whom the arch instance is Alec D'Urberville, the un-
abashed rake. Fitzpiers, Wildeve, and Troy belong in
this group, though each has certain traits that partially redeem him: Fitzpiers his intellectual attain-
ments, Wildeve (meanly though he has lived) the un-
hesitating courage of his last moments, Troy a certain
picturesque dash and touch of romance. In Boldwood, Henchard, and Farfrae the sexual emotion up-
surges through the stratum of interest in their professional pursuits. On the other side are the rigid
intellectualists like Knight and Angel Clare who err
in the reverse direction. The selfishness of this type
of man is best illustrated by the character of Swithin
St. Cleeve, the young astronomer in *Two on a Tower*.
Between the two extremes comes the Aristotelean
mean, the honest middle group, the men who are not
passion's slaves but who subordinate desire to the
other demands of life, who have the power, in Hardy's

words, "of keeping not only judgement but emotion suspended in difficult cases." There is of necesity less variety in this type than among the sensualists. These men are Wordsworthian in quality. They are able to subdue personal aspirations and to regard self-gratification as secondary in importance to their task of service. Through service they pay homage to the beloved object. Such men are John Loveday, Gabriel Oak, Giles Winterborne. It is of the last of these that Hardy says: "How little acquirement and culture weigh beside sterling personal character!" It is in his portrayal of men of this stamp that the best evidence lies for what has, perhaps paradoxically, been called "the optimism of Thomas Hardy." Fortuitously or otherwise Life has produced beings with courage, resourcefulness, patience, endurance, clearsightedness, tenderness, tolerance, forbearance, and unselfishness. The admiration lavished upon them and the elaborate care employed in their portrayal are the proper answer to the foolish and uncritical opinion that Hardy is scornful of human nature.

Shakespeare, Molière, Scott, Balzac, Dickens, and in less degree such writers as Fielding and Thackeray — each offers us a world filled with contrasting types of men and women. Their art is expended upon the realization of the infinite number of minute differences between individuals. Hardy, on the contrary, seeks to show how closely akin all men are. He thus reduces to a minimum individual differences and emphasizes the traits that are possessed in common by all. Hence, as compared with these older masters and from this point of view, his is the merest fragment of a world. The eccentricities of individuals are levelled out into a general humanity, moved by a common basic impulse, and suffering, each person in his way, from the fundamental fact of the tragedy of the conflict of reason and instinct. How severe the tragedy, or how merciful the mitigation of it, depends in part upon whether impulse be given free rein or be held in check.

6

The Poems

P O E T R Y has a way of outlasting prose, and though
there are still good judges who deny to Hardy equal
rank as a poet with that which he holds as a novelist,
though his poetry has not yet obtained the universal
recognition to which it is entitled, and though several of the novels have as good a chance of " immortality " as any fiction of the last half-century, nevertheless the " concise and quintessential expression "
attained by rhythmic form makes it likely that in
Hardy's case, as in Meredith's, the poetry will outlast
the prose, though Time will do its accustomed win-
nowing.

The volume of *Wessex Poems* was published at
a fortunate time. Had verses that enunciated clearly
the view of life that is only implicit in the earlier
novels been issued at the beginning of Hardy's career,
they would, in the words of Darwin's illustrious
predecessor, have " anticipated twenty or thirty years
of the march of honest feeling." They would have
met with the same indifferent or hostile reception

that was the lot of *The City of Dreadful Night*. At the close of the century not only was Hardy famous and therefore not only were verses of his likely to arouse curiosity, but honest feeling was better prepared for such poems as " Hap," and " Heiress and Architect," and " The Impercipient." The reader must be reminded that even before *Wessex Poems* appeared (1898) Hardy had laid down the general plan of *The Dynasts*, the first part of which appeared in 1903, the second in 1906, and the third and last in 1908. Some survey of the short poems may precede consideration of the epic-drama.

It surprised many people when Hardy, a novelist of established reputation, branched out into a field of work that, so far as the public knew, was almost untried. It is not surprising, of course, to those who know his history. At no time in his career did he wholly give over the writing of verse; especially remarkable, for example, are the " Poems of Pilgrimage " written in 1887. Early dates are attached to many poems published lately, and below many others one finds the legend " From an old note." What is extraordinary is that there was little or no falling-off in power in the successive volumes of meditative, narrative, and lyrical verse. The gnomic utterance, the compressed expression of a definite thought, the clumsiness that comes from conscientious grappling with subjects rebellious to form, the intensity of feeling, the wistful melancholy alternating with harsh irony, the sympathy beneath the cynicism, the quiet melody underlying the ruggedness — these are qualities of the earliest poems that one finds still present in the poems of latest date.

The technique is often rugged, sometimes faulty; but few of the various poets endowed with a more melodious ear have had Hardy's wealth of themes. A harsh and halting presentation of keenly imagined situation, sharply felt emotion, sternly confronted opinion, has claims upon our attention and admiration as strong as those exerted by the melodists. Not that I would imply that Hardy's technique is always below the level of his ideas. On the contrary it is frequently completely successful in its unobtrusive melody, winding through a wide variety of stanzaic forms, compelling rhymes to its service, and often depending upon some faintly remembered cadence of Dorsetshire folk-rhythm.

Why has Hardy written verses that are often cynical, satiric, ironic, sinister; often despairing; almost always melancholy and disillusioned? If, as he says,

> Faiths by which my comrades stand
> Seem fantasies to me,

were it not better done as others use, to rest in silence, and to leave, as a very different poet has counselled, unquestioning faith to those who find comfort and support therein? The answer is twofold. "B.V." phrased it in the proem to *The City of Dreadful Night:*

Because a cold rage seizes at one at whiles
To show the bitter, old and wrinkled truth
Stripped naked of all vesture that beguiles,
False dreams, false hopes, false masks and modes of
    youth;
Because it gives some sense of power and passion
In helpless impotence to try to fashion
Our woe in living words howe'er uncouth.

It is, in other words, in the first place the instinct of
the artist, seeking expression; and, in the second, the
feeling that Truth for its own sake is to be prized
" though a whole celestial Lubberland were the price
of Apostasy." Huxley speaks in one of his letters of
the satisfaction derived from " the sense of having
worked according to one's capacity and light, to
make clear and get rid of cant and shams of all sorts."
To those whom such work alarms and offends Hardy
answers in the words of Saint Jerome: " If an offence
come out of the truth, better it is that the offence
come than that the truth be concealed." This is the
burden of Hardy's dignified sonnet " To a Lady, Of-
fended by a Book of the Writer's." And the thought
often occurs that the poet and those who think like
him are but the precursors towards a point of view
that will be ever more generally approached as time
goes on. His sense of the toughness of the battle in this
righteous cause is voiced in the verses written in Gib-
bon's garden at Lausanne:

Thomas Hardy

A spirit seems to pass,
Formal in pose, but grave withal and grand:
He contemplates a writing in his hand,
And far lamps fleck him through the thin acacias.

Anon the leaves are closed,
With " It is finished! " And at the alley's end
He turns, and when on me his glances bend
As from the Past comes speech — small, muted, yet
composed.

" How fares the Truth now? — Ill?
— Do pens but slily further her advance?
May one not speed her but in phrase askance?
Do scribes aver the Comic to be Reverend still?

" Still rule those minds on earth
At whom sage Milton's wormwood words were
hurled:
' Truth like a bastard comes into the world
Never without ill-fame to him who gives her
birth '? "

Hardy is not didactic; he has no desire to force
opinions upon others; he puts forward a series of personal impressions, set down at different times, under
different circumstances, and in widely contrasting
moods. Like Thomson, he writes, not for the young,
nor for those who "grow fat among the shows of
life," nor for

pious spirits with a God above them
To sanctify and glorify and love them;

and only in rare moments for "sages who foresee a
heaven on earth." "None uninitiate" will compre-

hend. Hence his particular appeal to the type of mind
that has been affected by the determinism so rife during the closing years of the nineteenth century. The
value for humanity at large lies in this: that Hardy's
poetry moots questions generally put beyond discussion, that it probes into conventions, that it stimulates
to a new estimation of old standards and symbols and
formulas. It has, of course, merits of another order,
for it stirs the emotions while it quickens the intellect,
else it would not be great verse.

Hardy's hope was that the poems " in dramatic,
ballad, and narrative form should include most of
the cardinal situations in social and public life, and
those in lyric form a round of emotional experiences
of some completeness." But he is fully aware of " the
little done, the undone vast," and in the poetry that
he composed, though its range is not so narrow as
some critics contend, he by no means covered all the
cardinal situations of life. Rather he tended to return
often to one or another of a few particular situations,
viewing them now from one angle and now from another.

The scene of most of the short poems is laid in
Wessex and the characters are often Wessex peas-
antry. But the application is general. In the essay on
" The Profitable Reading of Fiction " he wrote:

All persons who have thoughtfully compared class
with class . . . are convinced that education has as yet
but little broken or modified the waves of human impulse
on which deeds and words depend. So that in the

portraiture of scenes in any way emotional or dramatic — the highest province of fiction — the peer and the peasant stand on much the same level.

This is equally true of narrative poetry. Accordingly universal human nature is portrayed in the particular guise of Wessex life. Some of the ballads and narrative pieces are cheerful in tone, occasionally quite rollicking: "The Bride-Night Fire," for example (one of the few poems, by the way, written in dialect), or "At Casterbridge Fair," or "The Homecoming" with its unexpectedly hopeful ending developing out of the dismal setting. But many others are pathetic or tragic, and of these a large number, as one would expect, deal with love-entanglements and marital difficulties. "The Burghers" suggests the situation of Sue Bridehead and Phillotson, for it is the tale of a husband who not only spares his unfaithful wife but allows her to leave him for her lover. The wife in " The Dame of Athelhall " repents of her rashness in running away from her husband with her lover and returns home secretly, only to overhear her husband congratulating himself on being rid of her. Irony of a lighter sort is used in " The Curate's Kindness," an amusing piece, the kindness being the curate's intercession with the workhouse authorities on behalf of an old couple, that they might live together instead of being placed in different wards; the irony being that the old man's hope which had reconciled him to the shame of the workhouse had been that there he would be separated from the forty years'

burden of his wife's company. A husband's temperament, the contrary of that portrayed in " The Burghers," is shown in the grim piece called " A Conversation at Dawn." A few poems — " The Duel," " The
Dark-Eyed Gentleman," and " One Ralph Blossom
Soliloquizes," for example — support the statement
that Hardy is moved to cheerfulness only by " the
triumphant indulgence in sexual desire." The cynicism of some pieces is so dark as to overreach itself
and touch on the farcical, as in many of the " Satires
of Circumstance," in " The Statue of Liberty," and
in the verses that begin " Ah, are you digging on my
grave? " In one such piece it is told how an admirer
of a great preacher peeps into the vestry-room after
the service and sees him re-enacting before the mirror
the gestures that had so moved his congregation; in
another, a lover, returning for his forgotten walking-
stick, overhears his sweetheart berating her mother
ferociously; in still another a stranger newly come to
town overhears a company in a bar-room telling
anecdotes of the past disreputable life of the woman,
well known in that locality, whom he has just married. In the " Apology " prefixed to *Late Lyrics and
Earlier* Hardy offered a defence, or rather an explanation, of these harsh and racy pieces which is acceptable in so far as it is admitted that they were inspired
by " a satirical and humorous intention." But such an
explanation hardly covers the question of the mere
good taste of certain pieces whose themes are beneath
the dignity of a great poet. But by contrast such

pieces reveal not only those qualities in which his genuine merit rests but also the qualities of great poetry, which never debases and sneers at human nature but which exalts and uplifts. To offset these cynical verses there are, fortunately, many others; passionate lyrics and meditative pieces that exhibit a deep realization of the lastingness and loyalty of love: "Her Immortality" and "Her Death and After" in *Wessex Poems,* or "The Clock-Winder" in *Moments of Vision.* This last poem, which illustrates his terseness, instinct for "atmosphere," halting music, and deep feeling, may be quoted.

It is dark as a cave,
Or a vault in the nave
When the iron door
Is closed and the floor
Of the church relaid
With trowel and spade.

But the parish-clerk
Cares not for the dark
As he winds in the tower
At the regular hour
The rheumatic clock,
Whose dilatory knock
You can hear when praying
At the day's decaying,
Or at any lone while
From a pew in the aisle.

Up, up from the ground
Around and around

The Poems

In the turret stair
He clambers, to where
The machinery is,
With its tick, click, whizz,
Deliberately measuring
Each day to its end
That mortal men spend
In sorrowing and pleasuring.
Nightly thus does he climb
To the trackway of Time.

Him I followed one night
To this place without light,
And, ere I spoke, heard
Him say, word by word,
At the end of his winding,
The darkness unminding: —

" So I wipe out one more,
My Dear, of the sore
Sad days that still be,
Like a drying Dead Sea,
Between you and me! "

Who she was no man knew:
He had long borne him blind
To all womankind;
And was ever one who
Kept his past out of view.

A like sense of the value of human kindliness is found
in many poems: " A Plaint to Man," " In a Wood "
(where such kindliness is contrasted with the cruelty
of Nature), and in that most beautiful of all Hardy's
lyrics, " To Meet or Otherwise ":

Thomas Hardy

Whether to sally and see thee, girl of my dreams,
        Or whether to stay
And see thee not! How vast the difference seems
        Of Yea from Nay
Just now. Yet this same sun will slant its beams
        At no far day
On both our mounds, and then what will the differ-
    ence weigh!

Yet I will see thee, maiden dear, and make
        The most I can
Of what remains to us amid this brake
        Cimmerian
Through which we grope, and from whose thorns we
    ache,
        While still we scan
Round our frail, faltering progress for some path or
    plan.

By briefest meeting something sure is won;
        It will have been:
Nor God nor Daemon can undo the done,
        Unsight the seen,
Make muted music be as unbegun,
        Though things terrene
Groan in their bondage till oblivion supervene.

So, to the one long-sweeping symphony
        From times remote
Till now, of human tenderness, shall we
        Supply one note,
Small and untraced, yet that will ever be
        Somewhere afloat
Amid the spheres, as part of sick Life's antidote.

The Poems

The harshness — one is tempted to say the hideousness and repulsiveness — of such poems as "The Newcomer's Wife," "The Rival," "The Statue of Liberty," and "The Dead and the Living" must not blind one to the fact that these things are transcripts from life where such things are possible or to the existence of other poems such as the two just quoted that present a contrasting view of things.

Two closely allied groups of poems have a particular "topical" interest. These are the verses inspired by the Boer War and those concerning the Great War of 1914–1918. In the earlier series there is not a sign of the jingoism that found its most characteristic expression in Kipling's poems or of that extravagant denunciation of the Boers that disgraced Swinburne. On the other hand there are no protests against the South African excursion of British Imperialism such as Sir William Watson and Wilfrid Scawen Blunt voiced in verse. Hardy's interest is not in rival policies and conflicting claims. He expresses the pathos of parting; the irony of the arrival of letters home after the news has been received of their writer's death; the loneliness of a northerner's grave under the southern stars; the joy of re-union. The foul anachronism of War "in this late age of thought and pact and code" is denounced, and he sees as a hopeful sign that the old view of War as a romantic adventure is dying out. "The Sick Battle-God" is an impressive rendering of this theme. In the later series the very uncharacteristic confidence in the perfect justice of England's cause suggests that Hardy may have been pressed into the propaganda service; but there is still a prevailing sense of the pathos of the break-down of efforts towards international goodwill. In the sonnet called "The Pity of It" he tells how he walked through Wessex lanes and heard "many an ancient word of local lineage" like "Thu bist," "Er war," "Ich woll"; and he curses those, whoever they be, who separated kin-folk, kin-tongued. Some of these poems of the war are obviously merely occasional; others are as characteristic of Hardy as any he ever composed. "In Time of 'The Breaking of Nations,'" for example, expresses the idea so frequently in his mind of the contrast between the apparently and the really great, between war's annals and falling dynasties, and the man at the plough, and the maiden and her lover who wander whispering by. The very powerful "Quid hic agis?" presents the poet's personal reaction to the conflict. His final judgement upon the world-upheaval is heard in "The Blow."

> That no man schemed it is my hope —
> Yea, that it fell by will and scope
>   Of That Which some enthrone,
> And for whose meaning myriads grope.
>
> For I would not that of my kind
> There should, of his unbiassed mind,
>   Have been one known
> Who such a stroke could have designed;

Since it would augur works and ways
Beneath the lowest that man assays
  To have hurled that stone
Into the sunshine of our days!

And if it prove that no man did,
And that the Inscrutable, the Hid,
  Was cause alone
Of this foul crash our lives amid,

I'll go in due time, and forget
In some deep graveyard's oubliette
  The thing whereof I groan,
And cease from troubling; thankful yet

Time's finger should have stretched to show
No aimful author's was the blow
  That swept us prone,
But the Immanent Doer's That does not know,

Which in some age unguessed of us
May lift Its blinding incubus,
  And see, and own:
" It grieves me I did thus and thus! "

With that practical meliorism which is the paradox
of his philosophy Hardy looks forward to an era of
international understanding.

The series of " Poems of Pilgrimage " and the
scattered elegies and memorial poems on various poets
are good examples of certain qualities of Hardy's
verse. Since Byron invented the form with *Childe
Harold* there have been innumerable poems of places.
Hardy has accomplished something in the same order

of subject-matter yet quite unlike other poems of the sort. This group of poems well shows how fertile Hardy is in ideas, how he has never had to cast around for themes as Tennyson so obviously did. He does not " sing but as the linnet sings " but because he has something definite to say, a clear-cut thought to express in rhythmic form. In the old theatre at Fiesole a child brings him an ancient coin; straightway he recognizes that he has discovered others of like stamp in Dorsetshire; and the vast panorama of European history and " the power, the pride, the reach of perished Rome " flash upon his mind. In " At the Pyramid of Cestius " he contrasts the seeming importance with the real importance of the Roman whose deeds are all forgotten but whose monument now serves to beckon pilgrim feet to the tombs of Shelley and Keats. In " Shelley's Skylark " one finds Hardy's favourite thought of the contrast between humble causes and often great effects, for somewhere in the neighbourhood of Leghorn where he writes there lies " a tiny pinch of priceless dust " which is all that remains of the lark that inspired Shelley to win " ecstatic heights in thought and rhyme." Other poems on poets are nearer to the formal elegy. One is the exceptionally beautiful elegy on Swinburne called " A Singer Asleep," an example of that sort of laudatory criticism in verse with which Swinburne himself so often experimented and of which Sir William Watson is the acknowledged master. It is remarkable for its apt appreciation of the poet's temperament

and particularly for its reminiscences of the stormy
reception of the *Poems and Ballads:*

> It was as though a garland of red roses
> Had fallen about the hood of some smug nun
> When irresponsibly dropped as from the sun,
> In fulth of numbers freaked with musical closes,
> Upon Victoria's formal middle time
>   His leaves of rhythm and rhyme.
>
> O that far morning of a summer day
> When, down a terraced street whose pavements lay
> Glassing the sunshine into my bent eyes,
> I walked and read with a quick, glad surprise
>   New words in classic guise, —
>
> The passionate pages of his earlier years,
> Fraught with hot sighs, sad laughters, kisses, tears;
> Fresh-fluted notes, yet from a minstrel who
> Blew them not naïvely, but as one who knew
>   Full well why thus he blew.

The last three lines are a sharp and exact estimate of
Swinburne's mood in 1866.

The latest written of this group of elegiac poems
is " To Shakespeare After Three Hundred Years." A
comparison of this poem with the other tributes gathered together in the tercentenary volume of homage
to Shakespeare brings out strikingly the originality
of Hardy's genius. He approaches even so well-worn
a theme from an angle that demonstrates his idiosyn-
crasy. The motive is once more the contrast between
the apparent and the real significance of human

endeavour. What did Shakespeare's fellow-citizens
know of his greatness? Hardy pictures two Stratford
men chatting together on the day of his death:

> " I'faith, few knew him much here, save by word,
> He having elsewhere led his busier life;
> Though to be sure he left with us his wife."
> — " Ah, one of the tradesmen's sons, I now recall . . .
> Witty, I've heard . . . .
> We did not know him. . . . Well, good-day.
> Death comes to all."

Many of Hardy's poems are broodings upon the
coming on of age, at times wistful, at times cynical.
The contrast between the passion of youth and the
faint relics of an old fire is what gives such extraordinary and pathetic quality to the amazing self-revela-
tory poems on his wife's death. Other such pieces are
" The Two Rosalinds," " The Revisitation," " Mid-
dle-Age Enthusiasms," and " Autumn in King's Hin-
tock Park." Many poems are meditations upon the
various aspects of death. Some of these pieces, as
would be expected, are among Hardy's most dis-
tinguished achievements in verse. The early poem
" Heiress and Architect," as we have seen, puts into
allegorical form the universal experience of disillu-
sion and decline and death. But he muses not only
upon the inevitability of death; he sees its dignity.
In a Casterbridge church pew are carved the initials
of three captains who went to the wars, only one of
whom returned. For a moment the survivor felt triumphant in the thought that only he had lived:

Yet saw he something in the lives
Of those who'd ceased to live
That sphered them with a majesty
Which living failed to give.

Transcendent triumph in return
No longer lit his brain:
Transcendence rayed the distant urn
Where slept the fallen twain.

And he senses the repose of death: *lieta no, ma sicura.*
" Jubilate " and " While Drawing in a Churchyard "
both tell of the experiences of living persons who
become aware of the contentment of the dead. In
the former weird poem it is told how the snow in
a churchyard becomes transparent one night and a
chance wanderer sees the dead below, foreshortened
as though he watched a stage from the gallery. They
are stepping a stately dance, singing meanwhile: " We
are out of it all! — yea, in Little-Ease cramped no
more! " In the other piece the yew tree is heard com-
menting upon the error of the living in misjudging
the lot of those " whom kindly earth secludes from
view ":

" They ride their diurnal round
Each day-span's sum of hours
In peerless ease, without jolt or bound
Or ache like ours. . . .

" ' Now set among the wise,'
They say: ' Enlarged in scope,
That no god trumpet us to rise
We truly hope.' "

The same motive is employed very touchingly in
"Friends Beyond," a poem in memory of Wessex
men of Hardy's youth-time. The only tragedy that
can touch the dead, he says in another mood, is their
defencelessness under misrepresentation. On a New
Year's Eve he hears the "Spectres That Grieve":

> "We are among the few death sets not free,
> The hurt, misrepresented names, who come
> At each year's brink, and cry to History
> To do them justice, or go past them dumb."

"Go past them dumb "— that is the fate that awaits
all but the greatest of men. It is "The Second Death."
In the poem of that title, in "The To-Be-Forgotten,"
in "His Immortality," and in the beautiful verses
"Her Immortality" Hardy applies to ordinary humanity the cold consolation offered by the Positivists,
the promise of life "on lips of other men." The be-
reaved lover, wandering through the meads, comes
to the place where he had seen his Beloved for the last
time, and there comes to him there a vision of her,
and in utter grief he cries that he will kill himself and
join her ghost. But she dissuades him, saying:

> "A Shade but in its mindful ones
> Has immortality;
> By living, me you keep alive,
> By dying you slay me."

The lover dismisses his distaste for life and promises
to guard himself from harms in order that her immortality in his memory may endure. But his grief

grows with the passage of years, for he knows that when he dies the second death will come to his Beloved.

Other poems connected by definite lines of thought might be grouped together. There are those of nature-description; poems of despair; poems in which there are traces of a strange hopefulness; many that present aspects of the Will that moves the universe; many that may be described as Cosmic Questionings. To leave them aside here is to risk giving a false impression of the range of Hardy's genius and poetic thought; but they may all be best considered in our final chapter as illustrations of Hardy's tentative metaphysic.

WHAT then, in sum, weighing the qualities of these miscellaneous short poems, may one say in support of the contention that Hardy must be reckoned among the great English poets? In the first place, though in his earlier poems there are some pieces (notably those in the sonnet form) that are obviously felicitous echoes of Shakespearean ideas and phraseology, his work is from first to last bound firmly together as the product of one strong mind, independent in style and thought. In the earliest poems there are anticipations of the latest. This is not to say that Hardy stood still. The development has been from the particular to the universal. His poetry shows abundantly the ability to sense " the abiding in the transient," the universal import of matters that on the face of them are of mere individual significance, the applicability of personal experiences to all men. Just as in many passages in the novels a curtain seems to rise for an instant and we see the vastness of things encompassing the human actors, so in the poems one finds very often a suggestion of larger issues than those that appear on the surface. The saddening thought that it was only by hap that the lover took the path that led him to his love, and that he might just as well have gone another way, suggests humanity enslaved to chance whether for happiness or for distress. The meeting with the " girl of my dreams " (in the poem quoted above) suggests the general " symphony of human tenderness " to which that meeting supplies one note. This poetry is impersonal in the sense that the issues involved are larger than personality; it is immensely personal in the impression it makes of profound emotion behind it. The sorrow, the anger, the cynicism, the despair, the faint flickering hope are Hardy's own; but they are more. Humanity itself is heard piping in fields and groves its solitary anguish. When we read these voicings of the pathos of unbelief, or of the lost enthusiasms of youth, or of the fading memories of the dead, or of the irony of the conflict between purposes and results, we mourn, not for the poet only who has experienced them, but for ourselves. What he offers is something besides technical mastery of verse or profundity of thought. The something further is in ourselves. Now from one facet and now from another he reflects the sorrow and hope of the ages. In quintessential form he voices human experience. Whether we accept the implications which he himself draws therefrom is not his concern; unlike nearly all his contemporaries he is not didactic. The " broken arc " may present to some minds the promise of the " perfect round " in another sphere of existence. Other minds may see with Hardy the quandary in which humanity labours. It is not the anger or the despair or the consolation of one Self that matters. Let each individual acquiesce or rebel according to his reaction to Circumstance. The Fact remains. It is this sense of the Fact that dominates Hardy's thought. Wordsworth, Shelley, Keats, Tennyson, Browning, Swinburne, Meredith — each presses upon us his solution of life; and each solution is satisfactory to some minds, rejected by others. Hardy does nothing of the kind. What he gives is a clear-sighted, determined facing and examination of the worst contingencies as well as of the best in the human condition. As in the novels, he poses questions, he confronts problems, he opens up new avenues of thought. He faces Fact; and not the separate isolated fact alone. Each experience is part of a larger one, in broadening circles till it embraces the Infinite. Thus are the Past and Present linked together, the meanest insect with the farthest star. Thus is a stellar gauge given wherewith to measure the place and pretensions of humanity. The Self — and this is the more remarkable because of the passionate practical individualism of the novels — is made subordinate to the Whole; the particular parcels of the Will are seen as portions of Its Immanence.

ᴜⲛᴜⲛᴜⲛᴜⲛᴜⲛᴜⲛⲟ

Turning now to *The Dynasts*, one must premise that the epic-drama is so charged with the full weight of Hardy's metaphysic that consideration of its philosophy must be postponed to the next and final chapter and that here we are concerned with it as a dramatic poem, a chronicle play on an enormous scale. Some years before he began the drama Hardy explained to the public why he did not attempt to write plays. But there is nothing surprising in the fact that at length he turned to that medium. Every considerable poet of the nineteenth century yielded at one time or another and to a greater or less extent to the lure of the drama. Moreover, there was always a kind of dramatic quality in Hardy's genius, as may be seen in the way in which his stories can be resolved into a succession of firmly articulated scenes.

It was said earlier in this study that the period of the Napoleonic Wars stamped a deep impression upon the memories of the people of Southern England and that Hardy grew up among relics and stories of that time. A group of short poems purposely left unconsidered in the previous sections of this chapter deals with Napoleonic themes. Of these pieces perhaps the most striking is " The Peasant's Confession." It is in the form of a dramatic monologue, a form

[162]

which may be regarded as the most typical genre contributed by the Victorian period to poetry. A dying peasant is imagined as telling the real circumstances of Grouchy's failure to keep Blücher away from Wellington according to the orders sent him by Napoleon before Waterloo. The tale is of course purely fanciful, but it illustrates again Hardy's idea of the great consequences that often flow from insignificant motives, for the peasant who guided the officer carrying Napoleon's dispatch learned from him that if Grouchy met Blücher the resultant battle would be fought over his own farm and to prevent its ruin he purposely misdirected the officer. Another poem, " Leipzig," is a narrative of the Battle of the Nations by a veteran of German descent living in Wessex. Several stanzas of this piece were afterwards introduced into corresponding scenes of *The Dynasts.* "The Alarm " is a tale founded on the rumour of Napoleon's successful landing on the Wessex coast, a report that is also introduced into *The Trumpet-Major* and into a very vivid scene in *The Dynasts.* The short story of " A Tradition of 1804 " tells of a shepherd who saw Napoleon and some of his staff land one night on the English coast to choose a fit landing place for the army that was in preparation across the Channel. The novel just named was Hardy's first considerable imaginative treatment of the period. He himself stated that on completing it he felt that he had touched only the fringes of the great subject. A foot-note in *The Dynasts* on the location in Brussels of the hall where the ball before Waterloo was held reveals the fact that as long ago as the seventies Hardy was an " enthusiast " on the subject of the Wars; and an old Note-book, dating also from the seventies, exists which contains a rough sketch of the plan of the epic-drama. In the preface to *The Dynasts* Hardy says that one motive for writing it was his conviction that England's share in the struggle had not been sufficiently emphasized in previous imaginative renderings of the theme. But behind any such patriotic motive and behind his life-long interest in the period was undoubtedly his chief purpose: the choice of the largest possible theatre of action whereon to exhibit all men in the grip of Circumstance, those on the topmost heights of human glory along with the peasants of the obscurest Wessex hamlet. *The Dynasts* thus illustrates explicitly and on the largest possible scale the deterministic philosophy inherent in the later novels. While entirely independent of them and to be judged for itself alone, it elaborates many hints and suggestions in the novels and shorter poems. Certain admirable scenes connect it with Wessex. It owes a good deal to the chronicle play of Elizabethan England; something to Stendhal; something to Hugo; something to Tolstoy's *War and Peace;* something to *Faust;* and a vast amount to patient study of contemporary source-material and of the researches of specialists. There are resemblances to Meredith's interpretation of Napoleon's character in the " Odes in Contribution to the Song of French History," but these are coincidences only for Hardy did not know these "Odes" till after the completion of *The Dynasts*. In the scene of the burial of Sir John Moore, Hardy successfully challenges comparison with one of the most popular of all English poems; in the scene of the Duchess of Richmond's ball, with Byron and Thackeray, to say nothing of *Charles O'Mally*. But though its antecedents can be traced out with some distinctness, *The Dynasts* remains a thing apart from other works of literature, a new and successful experiment and departure. The first instalment was greeted with mingled praise and doubt; but from the time of the appearance of Part Three it has grown in reputation and is now held by all good judges to be the greatest work of literature produced during this generation, grand in scope, profound in thought, sure and subtle in grasp.

The historic period covered by *The Dynasts* is ten years: from Napoleon's coronation at Milan and the renewal of the war in 1805 to his final defeat at Waterloo. The first part is concerned mainly with England's checking of Napoleon at Trafalgar and the Emperor's triumphant course upon the Continent to the climax of Austerlitz. The second presents the overthrow and humiliation of Prussia, the development of the Peninsular Campaign, and the efforts of Napoleon to establish his dynasty firmly upon the throne of France through the divorce of Josephine and the marriage to Maria Louisa of Austria. The third part exhibits the Russian campaign and disaster, the battle of Leipzig, Napoleon's first abdication, the Congress of Vienna, the escape from Elba, and the final campaign of Waterloo. The scenes of each part are thus grouped around a few outstanding events: Trafalgar and Austerlitz; Jena, Wagram, the Peninsular Campaign, and the divorce of Josephine; Moscow, Leipzig, Elba, and Waterloo. The reaction of ordinary life, in high and low degree, to these stupendous activities is shown in a great variety of scenes in London, Paris, Madrid, Berlin, Moscow — and Wessex. The domestic troubles and intrigues of Napoleon, of the Queen of Spain, and of the Prince Regent; the private conferences and burdens of ministers of state; the " grim romance of war" as experienced by the private soldier and by the stragglers behind the armies; and the faint, confused reflex of far-off events in the minds of the Wessex peasantry are all portrayed. The action at times descends to the point of view of some Parisian salon or London ball-room or theatre, or Parliamentary debate, or wretched hut in which straggling soldiers find shelter, or metropolitan street in which stodgy citizens congregate, or remote Wessex heath where beacon-keepers hold their watch. And again the action soars aloft to the " Over-World " whence all Europe can be surveyed, stretched out in an insignificance whereon whole armies move like crawling worms and individuals of greatest moment, humanly speaking, are reduced to meanest humility.

The various scenes differ as markedly in their interest as in their method of presentation. It has been said by some critics that the parliamentary debates and diplomatic discussions are dull — but is not that true of such debates and discussions in actuality? Again it has been said that the battle-scenes are over-numerous, one crowding upon the other, too unrelieved in horror — who living between 1805 and 1815 would have denied that such was the reality of war? As in the novels, so in *The Dynasts* it is easy to perceive where Hardy is not fired by his subject and is the conscientious workman rather than the inspired poet. But without exception he rises magnificently to the great occasions that his theme so frequently presents. The death of Nelson and the battle of Austerlitz; the interview between Napoleon and the Queen of Prussia, when he gives her the rose in lieu of Magdeburg; the retreat to Coruña and the burial of Sir John Moore; the announcement to Josephine of the planned divorce; the burning of Moscow; Leipzig; and the entire group of scenes that depict the battle of Waterloo — all are incomparably vivid, grasping alike the largest implications and the most minute details of the events. Yet quite as memorable are many of the scenes that present side-issues of the Clash of Peoples. One may call to mind the alarm in Wessex over the rumoured landing of the French and that other Wessex scene of the burning of Napoleon's effigy; the comments of the London citizens with which the Trafalgar act closes (here Hardy introduces the grim tradition of the " broaching " of the cask in which Nelson's body was brought home); the squalid huts wherein lie deserters from Wellington's army in Spain; the scene depicting the insane George the Third in the care of his physicians; the gala performance at the opera in honour of the Czar's visit to London, when the mob hoots at the Regent and cheers the wronged Queen; the death of the frozen soldiers on the Russian plains; the ball before Waterloo; the scene in the women's camp behind the English army during the progress of the last great battle. There is but one strange omission from this great panorama of life, and that omission the student of literature must always regret. Statesmen, soldiers, seamen, lawyers, physicians, men and women of all classes of society from emperor to yokel, from queen to prostitute, find their place here; but no representative of the world of letters. Yet this was the age of Goethe, Wordsworth, and Chateaubriand; and in 1815 Byron's dominance of the English imagination rivalled Napoleon's. Except for this all life sweeps by us. We have used the word " panorama " — it is Hardy's own modest term — but there is detail and order and grasp and unity such as no panorama could give. *The Dynasts* is an epic-drama of humanity — of humanity in its grandeur and its humility. In reading it one is constantly reminded of the great sentence in *Sartor Resartus:* " Thus, like some wild-flaming, wild-thundering train of Heaven's Artillery, does this mysterious Mankind thunder and flame, in long-drawn, quick-succeeding grandeur, through the unknown Deep."

And of that other sentence: "Napoleon, too, and his Moscow Retreats and Austerlitz Campaigns! Was it all other than the veriest Spectre-hunt; which has now, with its howling tumult that made night hideous, flitted away?"

It would be interesting, were there room in this brief study, to consider in some detail Hardy's interpretation of Napoleon, and to compare his portrayal of the Emperor with that of other poets. One can but offer a few suggestions. The closest analogy to Hardy's portrait is that in Meredith's ode "Napoleon." Meredith's analysis is not more subtle though it is decidedly less lucid. Sections nine and ten of the ode deal with the relations of Napoleon and France: his love for her, "more than little, less than much," as the tempered weapon with which he hewed through all impediments; the limitations of his ambitions; the pettiness and selfishness behind the grandeur and unscrupulousness. Hardy's own view of him is summed up in the magnificent last soliloquy of the Emperor after Waterloo, which is too long to quote entire and from which excerpts could not be made without doing injury to the impression made by the entire speech. A comparison might also be made with Lord De Tabley's fine and too-little-known ode "Napoleon the Great" which presents a similar analysis and which in like fashion contrasts the deeds of the Emperor, world-shaking yet transient, with the quiet and enduring English country-side. It may not be amiss to say that the present writer has received statements from more than one specialist in the field of Napoleonic research endorsing heartily the historical accuracy and psychological insight of Hardy's picture of the Emperor.

The historical or chronicle play is, as it were, a play-within-the-play, for the human action is watched over by a crowd of great Intelligences that range above this mortal state and that embody the various possible attitudes of the mind towards life — the passionless wisdom of the ages, the cynicism of despair, the fluctuating nervous pity of the human heart. To these spirits is given the function of providing the essential comment upon life, upon man, and upon the Power that moves mankind and the natural world alike; and in their elaborate massive debates Hardy has set forth his ripest views of the world and has accomplished his grandest poetry. They are spectators above the smoke and stir of this dim spot called earth and from their place of vantage are able to magnify seemingly small matters to the size warranted by their significance to mankind, and to minimize great events to the pettiness they assume when measured by infinity. They move with the swiftness of thought from place to place; mists, cloud-curtains, rain, and darkness shut off the human tragedy as the scenes close.

The language of *The Dynasts* has not received the general praise accorded to the strength and vividness of its imaginative presentation of the action. It varies from scene to scene, becoming conscientious and plodding when the action drags, rising to majestic heights when the subject inspires it. Of what great poem may not this be said? As one would expect from a perusal of the novels, the dialogue in the soldier and peasant scenes is uniformly racy and realistic. There is a swift and confident control of the vernacular in all the scenes of low life; there is a less certain mastery of society-talk. The parliamentary debates, military orders and proclamations, and diplomatic documents are tedious only because the original archives from which they are transcribed with just so much change as was necessary to put them into verse-form are tedious also. But over and over again the language is not only adequate (an adjective that damns with faint praise) but transcendently fine, the utterance exhibiting that perfect sensing of a situation which Watts-Dunton called "absolute vision." One of the many excellent instances of this is a passage drawn from the scene on the *Victory* where Nelson lies dying:

Nelson (*suddenly*): What are you thinking that you
    speak no word?

Hardy (*waking from a short reverie*):

Thoughts all confused, my lord: — their needs on
    deck,
Your own sad state, and your unrivalled past;
Mixed up with flashes of old things afar —
Old childish things at home, down Wessex way;
In the snug village under Blackdon Hill
Where I was born. The tumbling stream, the garden,

The placid look of the grey dial there,
Marking unconsciously this bloody hour,
And the red apples on my father's trees,
Just now full ripe.

Here there is the same feeling that we have already noted so often, of the close interconnection of all human things, the humblest with the greatest, Trafalgar with Blackdon Hill.

Or note the Dantesque directness, mingled with simplicity and power, of the report of a Russian soldier to his general concerning the French soldiers found dead around an extinguished camp-fire:

They all sit
As they were living still, but stiff as horns;
And even the colour has not left their cheeks,
Whereon the tears remain in strings of ice.—
It was a marvel they were not consumed:
Their clothes are cindered by the fire in front,
While at their backs the frost has caked them hard.

Or consider, finally, these indescribably solemn words of the Spirit of the Years to Napoleon after Waterloo:

Worthless these kneadings of thy narrow thought,
Napoleon; gone thy opportunity!
Such men as thou, who wade across the world
To make an epoch, bless, confuse, appal,
Are in the elemental age's chart
Like meanest insects on obscurest leaves
But incidents and grooves of Earth's unfolding;
Or as the brazen rod that stirs the fire
Because it must.

The Poems

There are charming lyrics in *The Dynasts:* "Budmouth Dears" and "My Love's Gone A-fighting," for example, or the song that closes the Trafalgar act. They are redolent of the war-spirit of a people, stressing emotion rather than thought. Some of them have been set to music. And many of the spirit-choruses are Hardy's highest performances in verse. It is impossible to name them all here, but one may recall the Albuera chorus in which the terror and pity and splendour of fiery gallantry are chanted; and the chorus (a rondeau — a new use for this old and in other poets' hands trivial form of verse) beginning "The skies fling flame on this ancient land"; and the Hymn of the Pities in the After-Scene; and the chorus before Waterloo — perhaps the most wonderful thing in the whole drama — beginning "The eyelids of eve fall together at last" — in which is voiced once more the close relationship of all things, the coneys and moles and worms and snails having their share in the sufferings that are about to fall upon the armies of France and of the allies.

7
"A Tentative Metaphysic"

M A N, in Hardy's novels and poems, becomes only one of the many phenomena of interest to the imaginative interpreter of life. The old anthropocentricity is gone. In a sonnet on the Matterhorn he muses upon the defiance with which the granite block has withstood the onset of centuries while events of tremendous import for poor humanity have had their day and ceased to be.

> Yet ages ere men topped thee, late and soon
> Thou didst behold the planets lift and lower;
> Saw'st, maybe, Joshua's pausing sun and moon,
> And the betokening sky when Cæsar's power
> Approached its bloody end; yea, even that Noon
> When darkness filled the earth till the ninth hour.

By implication this contrast is impressively set forth at the close of *A Group of Noble Dames* when, the stories all told and the club members departed to their homes, darkness reigns over the room in the museum where they had met:

"A Tentative Metaphysic"

The curator locked up the rooms, and soon there was only a single pirouetting flame on the top of a single coal to make the bones of the ichthyosaurus seem to leap, the stuffed birds to wink, and to draw a smile from the varnished skulls of Vespasian's soldiery.

So also in the otherwise nearly negligible novel *Two on a Tower* the feverishness of human passion is set impressively against a background of starry distances. Says the young astronomer to his mistress:

" The actual sky is a horror. . . . You would hardly think, at first, that horrid monsters lie up there waiting to be discovered. . . . Monsters to which those of the oceans bear no sort of comparison. . . . Impersonal monsters, namely, Immensities. Until a person has thought out the stars and their interspaces, he has hardly learnt that there are things much more terrible than monsters of shape, namely, monsters of magnitude without known shape. Such monsters are the voids and waste places of the sky."

Swithin's very words find echoes in one of the great discourses of the Spirit of the Years in *The Dynasts*.

A meditation upon a lunar eclipse takes the form of contrasting the petty pretentiousness of our concerns —

Nation at war with nation, brains that teem,
Heroes, and women fairer than the skies —

with the imperturbable serenity of the segment of shadow cast upon the moon, that sole stellar gauge of the real worth of " Heaven's high human scheme."

" A thousand years in Thy sight " — so Hardy seems
to address the Will — " are but as yesterday." The
monsters of the eocene become companions of man.
The Napoleonic Wars dwindle in that scale to micro-
scopic insignificance. In the After-Scene of *The Dynasts* the Spirit of the Years utters the necessary
comment:

> Yet but one flimsy riband of Its web
> Have we here watched in weaving — web Enorme,
> Whose furthest hem and selvage may extend
> To where the roars and plashings of the flames
> Of earth-invisible suns swell noisily,
> And onwards into ghastly gulfs of sky,
> Where hideous presences churn through the dark —
> Monsters of magnitude without a shape,
> Hanging amid deep wells of nothingness.

Thus viewed, Christianity becomes " a local thing "

> Beyond whose span, uninfluenced, unconcerned,
> The systems of the suns go sweeping on
> With all their many-mortaled planet train
> In mathematic roll unceasingly.

Men — whole nations — are moved like figures on a
lantern-slide, drawn to and fro by the halyards of the
all-pervading Will, the intertwisted strands of which
are revealed in certain scenes of *The Dynasts* to the
on-looking Intelligences. And the grandest phenomena of Nature, though they reduce to insignificance
the wildest turmoil of humanity, are no more free.
In the poem called " The Subalterns " the leaden sky,

the north wind, disease and death, disclaim responsibility for the functions which they are compelled
to perform.

Some few men, Napoleon among them, discern
the workings of the Will that harries them on, ful-
filling or baffling that which they imagine to be their
own purposes. Yet in the act of planning they are as
much under compulsion as in outward action. The
Power that moves the universe is shadowed forth
under a variety of august names: The High Influence,
the Eternal Urger, the Rapt Determinator, the Immanent Unreckoning, the Great Foresightless, the
Unconscious. As in the scheme of things adumbrated
by Schopenhauer, phenomena, in all their multi-
plicity, are but the appearances which hide the one
reality, the Will. It is to this Primal Force that in the
final analysis all the shows of the world reduce themselves; Man is but the highest expression of It. In lines
that have already become famous Hardy describes the
way in which It works:

> In the Foretime, even to the germ of Being,
> Nothing appears of shape to indicate
> That cognizance has marshalled things terrene,
> Or will (such is my thinking) in my span.
> Rather they show that, like a knitter drowsed,
> Whose fingers play in skilled unmindfulness,
> The Will has woven with an absent heed
> Since life first was; and ever will so weave.

So speaks the Spirit of the Years, representative of
the insight and experience of the ages. A number of

the shorter poems are concerned with cosmic questionings, some of them in the form of colloquies with God in which, with a boldness that suggests the work of Mr. James Stephens and other younger poets, Hardy presents an indictment of the faith in an anthropomorphic deity. Perhaps some primeval disaster cleft the original scheme of things apart. Perhaps the Will's "mindlessness of earthly woes" may be due to Its interest in other worlds, being wearied out with the ceaseless turmoil of earth. Perhaps the Godhead is dying downward, heart and brain all gone save for the last flicker of consciousness that abides in man. Or maybe man's consciousness is a foretoken of coming consciousness directing all things everywhere.

> Men gained cognition with the flux of time,
> And wherefore not the Force informing them?

Through some accident that rests unexplained mankind, "emerging with blind gropes from impercipience by listless sequence," has achieved consciousness and a moral sense.

> Our incorporeal sense,
> Our overseeings, our supernal state,
> Our readings Why and Whence,
> Are but the flower of Man's intelligence;
> And that but an unreckoned incident
> Of the all-urging Will, raptly magnipotent.

A sentence towards the end of *Jude the Obscure* anticipates precisely and succinctly the philosophy of *The Dynasts:*

"A Tentative Metaphysic"

Vague and quaint imaginings had haunted Sue . . . that the world resembled a stanza or melody composed in a dream; it was wonderfully excellent to the half-aroused intelligence, but hopelessly absurd at the full waking; that the First Cause worked automatically like a somnambulist, and not reflectively like a sage; that at the framing of the terrestrial conditions there seemed never to have been contemplated such a development of emotional perceptiveness among the creatures subject to those conditions as that reached by thinking and educated humanity.

The little poem called "In a Wood" contains the very crux of Hardy's tentative metaphysic. It recites such evidences of strangled aspiration, thwarted desire and blind conflict as those noted also in *The Woodlanders:* gnarled trunks, twisted branches, stunted growths, and bare and blighted ground (for Hardy never errs, as does Dickens, by imputing his own kindliness to the scheme of things.) These evidences lead the poet to this conclusion:

> Since, then, no grace I find
> Taught me of trees,
> Turn I back to my kind,
> Worthy as these.
>
> There at least smiles abound,
> There discourse trills around,
> There, now and then, are found
> Life-loyalties.

Captious critics always note Hardy's inconsistency in ascribing to a purposeless and conscienceless Will the creation of beings in whom purpose and conscience have been evolved. But those critics are in error who accuse him of unawareness of this inconsistency. On the contrary he returns again and again to meditations upon " the intolerable antilogy of making figments feel."

How the faculty of reason came about is inexplicable; but it exists. Henceforth, for good or ill, two natures contend within man's bosom. For Hardy falls short of complete acceptance of the materialistic monism which he so often affirms. In humankind there is a struggle between intuition, the Will-to-Live, which is in accord with the blind Immanence that exists only for the sake of existing, and intellect, the Will-Not-to-Live, which knows that existence is not worth prolonging. We have found this doctrine expressed in almost allegorical form in *Jude the Obscure*. The connection with von Hartmann's Philosophy of the Unconscious is obvious. In the rivalry between Being and Not-Being the Will is still in control, but the power of Reason is growing and will one day prevail. Then the problem will be solved by a voluntary lapse into unconsciousness. Man will be healed of the wound of living.

Were this Hardy's final word his would indeed be " a twilight view of life." What more may be said? Can any contradiction to this view be found in his writings? Little at best, and that little must be weighed against the many evidences of revolt and despair. But at least he seems to hesitate upon the brink, and with a sacrifice of logic introduces among

the crashing chords of his pessimism a note of hope.
What if his view of life be the result of limited vision?
"The Darkling Thrush," that beautiful poem, describes a gaunt, wintry country-side from amidst
which in the gathering gloom there bursts forth the
full-hearted even-song of a bird:

> So little cause for carollings
>   Of such ecstatic sound
> Was written on terrestrial things
>   Afar or nigh around,
> That I could think there trembled through
>   His happy good-night air
> Some blessed Hope, whereof he knew
>   And I was unaware.

And even if his interpretation of life *is* sound? Hope
still resides in the possibility that the process that has
led life up from the primal ooze to man may be yet
functioning so that in the far future a conscious sympathy may form a link between the Will and Its
creatures. The awakening of consciousness, which
seems the bitterest whim of the Will — may that not
be the first stirrings in man of a power for good that
will one day permeate the vast framework of things?

> By some still close-cowled mystery
> We have reached feeling faster than he,
> But he will overtake us anon,
>   If the world goes on.

So Hardy wrote in a recently published " Fragment ";
and it is noteworthy that the masculine pronoun is

restored in this allusion to the Fundamental Energy. Elsewhere he expresses his awareness of

> That enkindling ardency from whose maturer glows
> The world's amendment flows.

And elsewhere still, in one of his grandest poems, the poet who so often shaped " weak phantasies " of the blind and dumb Willer raises his voice in praise because here and there old wrongs are dying out. Is there no hopefulness in this? Can it be that a " ripening rule " will transcend the " ancient rote-restricted ways,"

> That listless effort tends
> To grow percipient with advance of days,
> And with percipience mends?

No concession to the wishes of the novel-reading public, such as suggested the " happy ending " of *The Return of the Native*, compelled Hardy to close *The Dynasts* as he did. It is of the utmost significance that the last word is given, not to the Spirit Sinister (the exponent of a cynical pessimism) nor to the Spirit of the Years (who interprets the events of the human tragedy in accordance with a strict determinism), but to the Spirit of the Pities, the symbol of human sympathy and of the undying fire, the unconquerable hope of humanity. If the evils suffered by those whom the Will quickens can be neither curbed nor cured (so the final chorus sings), then let the Will darken swiftly to extinction. But the chorus ends otherwise:

"A Tentative Metaphysic"

But — a stirring thrills the air
Like to sounds of joyance there
    That the rages
    Of the ages
Shall be cancelled, and deliverance offered from the
    darts that were,
Consciousness the Will informing, till It fashion all
    things fair.

The events of the Great War might have been
employed by this sombre thinker as unqualified illustrations of the truth of a deterministic philosophy;
and indeed, as we have seen, he attaches the blame to
no man but rather to " the Immanent Doer That does
not know." But again the final word has hope in it,
for the Thing responsible for the dire crash

    . . . in some age unguessed of us
    May lift Its blinding incubus,
        And see, and own:
    " It grieves me I did thus and thus."

And the " Men who march away " are upheld by the
faith within them that " Victory crowns the just."
Hardy's grandest gift is that " double vision " of
which one of his best critics has spoken, whereby,
while seeing life as trivial and futile, he can see it also
as heroically sublime. The universe is not hopeless of
betterment that has produced the sort of men to
whom Hardy gives his meed of praise — and that has
produced the sympathy and tenderness with which he
cries, not to Tess only but to all humanity, " Poor
wounded name, my bosom as a bed shall lodge thee! "

BIBLIOGRAPHY

For details, see the works by Danielson, Esdaile and Webb listed below. In compiling this brief bibliography I have made special use of Mr. Esdaile's work and to him I wish to express my sense of obligation.

Collected Editions

(1) The Wessex Novels. First published by Osgood, McIlvaine and Co., 1895; continued by Harper Brothers and then by Macmillan and Co., with uniform volumes of the poems.

(2) A cheaper edition, often referred to as the " Uniform Edition," 1902 f. London: Macmillan; New York: Harper.

(3) The Pocket Edition. (A reissue of the " Uniform Edition " on India paper.) 1906 f. London: Macmillan; New York: Harper.

(4) The Wessex Edition. 1912 f. London and New York: Macmillan. This contains a new General Preface, Prefaces to each volume; and a few foot-notes. Originally complete in twenty volumes; supplementary volumes have been issued containing works written or first collected since 1912.

(5) The Mellstock Edition. 1921–22. London and New York: Macmillan. A limited *édition de luxe* now procurable only at a high premium.

Bibliography

The Novels and Romances

The following list is in chronological order. In the Wessex and Mellstock Editions the novels and romances are rearranged under four general headings: I. Novels of Character and Environment; II. Romances and Fantasies; III. Novels of Ingenuity; IV. Mixed Novels. (This last division is an after-thought, to include *A Changed Man,* etc., an *omnium gatherum* of miscellaneous pieces of slight importance first published collectively in 1913.)

1871. *Desperate Remedies.* London: Tinsley Brothers.

1872. *Under the Greenwood Tree.* London: Tinsley Brothers.

1873. *A Pair of Blue Eyes.* London: Tinsley Brothers. (First published serially in *Tinsley's Magazine,* September, 1872–July, 1873.)

1874. *Far from the Madding Crowd.* London: Smith, Elder and Co. (First published serially in *Cornhill Magazine,* January–December, 1874.)

1876. *The Hand of Ethelberta.* London: Smith, Elder and Co. (First published serially in *Cornhill Magazine,* July, 1875–May, 1876.)

1878. *The Return of the Native.* London: Smith, Elder and Co. (First published serially in *Belgravia,* January–December, 1878.)

Bibliography

1880. *The Trumpet-Major*. London: Smith, Elder and Co. (First published serially in *Good Words*, January–December, 1880.)

1881. *A Laodicean*. London: Sampson, Low, Marston and Co. (First published serially in *Harper's Magazine*, European Edition, December, 1880–December, 1881.)

1882. *Two on a Tower*. London: Sampson, Low, Marston and Co. (First published serially in *The Atlantic Monthly*, January–December, 1882.)

1886. *The Mayor of Casterbridge*. London: Smith, Elder and Co. (First published serially in *The Graphic*, January 2–May 15, 1886.)

1887. *The Woodlanders*. London: Macmillan and Co. (First published serially in *Macmillan's Magazine*, May, 1886–April, 1887.)

1888. *Wessex Tales: Strange, Lively and Commonplace*. London: Macmillan and Co. (First published serially at various dates between 1879 and 1888 in various magazines. In 1894 " An Imaginative Woman " was added to this collection. In the Wessex Edition of the the Collected Works two stories — " A Tradition of Eighteen Hundred and Four " and " The Melancholy Hussar " — were transferred to this collection from *Life's Little Ironies*, and " An Imaginative Woman " was transferred from this collection to *Life's Little Ironies*.)

Bibliography

1891. *Tess of the D'Urbervilles.* London: Osgood, Mc-Ilvaine and Co. (First published serially, in the main, in *The Graphic,* July 4–December 26, 1891. An episode, "The Midnight Baptism," appeared in *The Fortnightly Review,* May, 1891; another, "Saturday Night in Arcady," in *The National Observer,* November 14, 1891.)

1891. *A Group of Noble Dames.* London: Osgood, Mc-Ilvaine and Co. (First published in the Christmas Number of *The Graphic,* 1890.)

1894. *Life's Little Ironies, a Set of Tales: With some Colloquial Sketches entitled A Few Crusted Characters.* London: Osgood, McIlvaine and Co. (The "Few Crusted Characters" were here published for the first time; the other tales had appeared in various periodicals at various dates between 1882 and 1893.)

1896. *Jude the Obscure.* London: Osgood, McIlvaine and Co. (The serial publication was begun under the title *The Simpletons* in *Harper's Magazine,* European Edition, December, 1894; continued in the same magazine, under the title *Hearts Insurgent,* January–November, 1895.)

1897. *The Well-Beloved.* London: Macmillan and Co. (First published serially, under the title *The Pursuit of the Well-Beloved,* in *The Illustrated London News,* October 1–December 17, 1892.)

1913. *A Changed Man, The Waiting Supper and Other Tales, concluding with The Romantic Adventures of*

Bibliography

a Milkmaid. London: Macmillan and Co. (These
" minor novels " appeared originally in various periodicals at various dates between 1881 and 1900. On
the bibliographical history of *The Romantic Adventures of a Milkmaid* see a note by J. W. Beach in *The
Nation* (N. Y.) XCIV (1912), 82–3.)

⅃⅃⅃⅃⅃⅃⅃⅃⅃⅃

Poetical Works

Collected Editions. Volumes of later date than 1912 have
been added to the Wessex Edition. Messrs. Macmillan
publish a complete edition of the miscellaneous poems
in one volume (1919) with *The Dynasts* complete in
a companion volume (1910).

Selections. Selected Poems of Thomas Hardy. "Golden
Treasury Series." London: Macmillan (1916). The
same selection appeared in fine format in a limited
edition issued in 1921 by Philip Lee Warner, Publisher to the Medici Society, in the series of " Ricardi
Press Books."

1898. *Wessex Poems and Other Verses*. New York and
London: Harper Brothers. (With thirty illustrations
by Thomas Hardy. A very few pieces had already
appeared in periodicals.)

1902. *Poems of the Past and the Present*. New York and
London: Harper Brothers. (Many pieces had already
appeared in periodicals.)

Bibliography

1903–6–8: *The Dynasts: An Epic-Drama of the Napoleonic Wars.* London: Macmillan and Co. In 1927 Messrs. Macmillan published a limited edition in fine format with etched frontispiece portrait by Francis Dodd.

1909. *Time's Laughing-stocks and Other Verses.* London: Macmillan and Co.

1914. *Satires of Circumstance: Lyrics and Reveries, with Miscellaneous Poems.* London: Macmillan and Co.

1917. *Moments of Vision and Miscellaneous Verses.* London: Macmillan and Co.

1922. *Late Lyrics and Earlier, with Many Other Verses.* London: Macmillan and Co.

1923. *The Famous Tragedy of the Queen of Cornwall at Tintagel in Lyonesse.* London: Macmillan and Co.

1925. *Human Shows, Far Phantasies, Songs and Trifles.* London: Macmillan and Co.

ᴜᴜᴜᴜᴜᴜᴜ

Minor Prose Writings

1865. " How I Built Myself a House," *Chambers' Journal,* March 18, 1865.

1878. " An Indiscretion in the Life of an Heiress," *New Quarterly Magazine,* April–October, 1878.

Bibliography

1878. "Dialect in Novels," *The Athenaeum,* November 30, 1878.

1879. "The Dorsetshire Labourer," *Longman's Magazine,* July, 1879.

1888. "The Profitable Reading of Fiction," *The Forum,* March, 1888.

1890. "Candour in English Fiction," *The New Review,* January, 1890.

1891. "The Science of Fiction," *The New Review,* April, 1891.

1892. "Why I don't Write Plays," *Pall Mall Gazette,* August 31, 1892.

1893. "Ancient Earthworks at Casterbridge," *English Illustrated Magazine,* Christmas Number, 1893.

1906. "Memories of Church Restoration," *Cornhill Magazine,* July, 1906.

1908. Preface and Glossorial Index to: *Select Poems by William Barnes.* London: Henry Frowde. (Cf. Hardy's review of Barnes's *Poems of Rural Life, New Quarterly Review,* October, 1879; and his obituary article on Barnes in *The Athenaeum,* October 16, 1886.)

A few notes and letters to the press are not included in the above list. Hardy, though urged by friends to do so, never collected these miscellaneous pieces into a volume. An unauthorized collection of all the items in my list together with several other pieces has been published recently. This is: *Life and Art. By Thomas Hardy. Essays, Notes and Letters collected for the First Time.* Edited by Ernest Brennecke, Jr. New York: Greenberg, 1925.

᠊᠊᠊᠊᠊᠊᠊᠊᠊᠊᠊

Authorities

The following list does not pretend to be exhaustive and is no more than a guide to further reading.

Abercrombie, Lascelles. *Thomas Hardy: A Critical Study.* New York: Mitchell Kennerley, 1912. (Reissued in somewhat abridged form by the Viking Press, 1927.)

Beach, Joseph Warren. *The Technique of Thomas Hardy.* Chicago: The University of Chicago Press, 1922.

Berle, L. W. *George Eliot and Thomas Hardy.* New York: Mitchell Kennerley, 1917.

Brennecke, Ernest, Jr. *Thomas Hardy's Universe: A Study of a Poet's Mind.* Boston: Small, Maynard and Co., 1924.

Brennecke, Ernest, Jr. *The Life of Thomas Hardy.* New York: Greenberg, 1925.

Chase, Mary Ellen. *Thomas Hardy from Serial to Novel.* Minneapolis: The University of Minnesota Press, 1927.

Child, Harold. *Thomas Hardy.* New York: Henry Holt and Co., 1916.

Bibliography

Cunliffe, J. W. *English Literature during the Last Half Century.* New York: The Macmillan Co., 1919. (Contains a chapter on Hardy.)

Danielson, Henry. *The First Editions of the Writings of Thomas Hardy and Their Values.* London: Allen and Unwin, 1916.

Duffin, H. C. *Thomas Hardy: A Study of the Wessex Novels.* Manchester: The University Press, 1916.

Esdaile, Arundell. A " Short Bibliography " appended to Harold Child's *Hardy.*

Freeman, John. *Moderns.* New York: Crowell, 1917. (See pages 103–159.)

Garwood, Helen. *Thomas Hardy: An Illustration of the Philosophy of Schopenhauer.* Philadelphia: J. C. Winston Co., 1911.

Grimsditch, H. B. *Character and Environment in the Novels of Thomas Hardy.* London: Wetherby, 1925.

Harper, C. G. *The Hardy Country: Literary Landmarks of Wessex.* London: A. & C. Black, 1904.

Heath, Sidney. *The Heart of Wessex.* Boston: D. Estes and Co., 1911.

Hedgcock, F. A. *Thomas Hardy: Penseur et Artiste.* Paris: Librairie Hachette, 1910.

Hopkins, R. T. *Thomas Hardy's Dorset.* London: C. Palmer, 1922.

Bibliography

Johnson, Lionel. *The Art of Thomas Hardy*. London: Elkin Matthews and John Lane, 1894 (reissued 1922.)

Lea, Hermann. *A Handbook of the Wessex Country of Mr. Hardy's Novels and Poems*. London: Kegan Paul, Trench, Trubner and Co., 1906.

Lea, Hermann. *Thomas Hardy's Wessex*. London: Macmillan and Co., 1913.

Macdonell, Annie. *Thomas Hardy*. London: Hodder and Stoughton, 1894.

Saxelby, F. O. *A Thomas Hardy Dictionary*. London: Routledge, n. d.

Symons, Arthur. *A Study of Thomas Hardy*. London: C. J. Sawyer, 1928.

Webb, A. P. *A Bibliography of Thomas Hardy*. London: Frank Hollings, 1916. (Exhaustive to date of publication, including " Critical Notices, Essays and Apprecations " of Hardy in books and periodicals.)

Whitfield, A. S. *Thomas Hardy: The Artist, the Man and the Disciple of Destiny*. London: Grant Richards, 1921.

Windle, B. C. A. *The Wessex of Thomas Hardy*. London: John Lane, 1906 (reissued 1925.)

INDEX

Index

Index

Index